DEFYING
the
ODDS

One man's struggle and victory
over mental illness and his wife
whose trust in God never failed

ZOE A. ONAH

Please note that Destiny Image Europe's publishing style capitalizes certain pronouns in Scripture that refer to the Father, Son, and Holy Spirit, and may differ from some Bible publishers' styles. Take note that the name satan and related names are not capitalized. We choose not to acknowledge him, even to the point of violating grammatical rules.

DESTINY IMAGE™ EUROPE srl
Via Maiella, 1
66020 San Giovanni Teatino (Ch) – Italy

"Changing the world, one book at a time."

This book and all other Destiny Image™ Europe books are available at Christian bookstores and distributors worldwide.

To order products, or for any other correspondence:

DESTINY IMAGE™ EUROPE srl
Via della Scafa, 29/14
65013 Città Sant'Angelo (Pe), Italy
Tel. +39 085 4716623 • +39 085 8670146
Email: info@eurodestinyimage.com
Or reach us on the Internet: www.eurodestinyimage.com

ISBN 13: 978-88-96727-30-0
ISBN 13 Ebook: 978-88-96727-40-9
For Worldwide Distribution, Printed in Italy
1 2 3 4 5 6/14 13 12 11

DEDICATION

For Sophia, you are the wisdom of God; and Isaac, our laughter. Both of you are God's battleaxes in these end times.

ACKNOWLEDGMENTS

First of all, I would like to say thank you to the Holy Spirit, my Extraordinary Strategist without whom I am nothing. You have truly beautified my life. My hand is ever ready to take the dictates from the heart of the Father. Thank You for the *mimshach!* I love You, God, immensely.

Thank you to Pastor Chris Oyakhilome PhD, president of LoveWorld Ministry (Christ Embassy), and his lovely wife Rev. Anita, whose ministry I belong to. Your anointed teachings mold me and give me hope in the Word of God. May God truly bless and prosper you in all you do and the countless lives you have touched.

Thank you to my spiritual father, Pastor Nelson Ngoka. Wow! A smile can change the destiny of one looking for answers. Thank you for your ceaseless encouragement and prayers "when the going got tough." Thank you for answering the call. I pray that God continues to bless you. Thank you to my spiritual mother, Sister Sandra Ngoka. You read me like a book. Thank you for leading me on the straight and narrow. Thanks for being a wonderful wife to Pastor Nelson. Special thanks and acknowledgments also go to Pastor Chuka Ibeachum and Pastor Val Ibeachum.

Thank you to my Dad and Mum, Dr. and Mrs. W. Lisk. You brought me into this world and trained me in the way I should go, so that when I am old I never depart from it. I love you both so much. Thank you, Mum, for your billions of intercessory prayers. You taught me that there are no words such as "I can't." You refused to give up! Thanks to my brother, Darrell—you are simply the best. Thanks to my wonderful in-laws. I am so happy to belong to a beautiful family who always make me feel special. I am blessed, truly! I would also like to thank my many friends, relatives, and people I have met along this journey in life. There are too many to mention, but you all lit a candle on the path that helped show me who I would become.

Thank you to all the wonderful ministers of God around the world for answering God's call. May God's anointing continue to increase in your life. Who knew how many of your books would train and carry me for such a time as this?

Acknowledgements also go to Destiny Image Europe and the editors for all the work put into publishing this book. You all have been great to work with. Together with the Lord, we are changing the world, one book at a time!

Last, and certainly not least, thank you to my wonderful husband Eze. God brought us together as part of His plan so we can touch many lives. I am truly glad I waited. I love you with all my heart.

ENDORSEMENTS

It is humbling and awe-inspiring to read how Eze and Zoe fought the good fight of faith against prolonged mental illness and stayed in that fight till they laid hold of the abundant life promised by Jesus. This beautifully written book teaches many lessons about the overcoming power of faith, patience, and trusting commitment to the Word of God. Thank you, Zoe and Eze, for sharing these intimate moments of your painful experiences and giving us the encouragement we need to know that no matter how hopeless things may seem, no matter how many setbacks we face, faith never fails. This book is not just an inspiring narrative, but a Word-filled resource showing "little steps" anyone may take in order to come out of the most challenging and troubling situations in life. I wept in some parts, celebrated with them in others. I highly recommend it.

Pastor Val Ibeachum
host of Impacting Your World, Loveworld TV

I have known Zoe and Eze for a long time and was able to watch their faith grow and overcome this challenge of mental illness. They stuck to the Word of God and surely they got their wonderful miracle. As a practicing doctor, I understand how to some people such would seem impossible, but with God all things are possible. Mental illness, which includes a spectrum of conditions from depression to schizophrenia, is like a life sentence, in most cases not medically curable but requiring a lifetime of drug therapy. This is a beautifully written book which illustrates that the Word of God works and that through faith you can change any situation. It is a must-read for anyone going through any challenge, be it health, financial, or spiritual. This book will make you realize that great miracles are still happening to this day.

Dr. Concilia Dipura
MBChB, DA, FRCA

Beautifully written. This book achieves a delectable balance between the world of mind disorders, the effects they have on lives, and the qualities of the human spirit which enable one to look beyond limitations. It draws in the readers and carries them along. It is difficult to put down once started, and manages to deal with mental illness in a manner which is neither overpowering nor overly sentimental. A wonderful read.

Bothwell Xavier
MD, MBA

Very rarely do we come across stories of people who were able to move on from mental illness to live an even more productive life. With this story, Zoe Onah offers hope to millions of mental health patients and their carers around the world—people who might have thought that there was no hope.

Adaobi Tricia Nwaubani
author of *I Do Not Come to You by Chance*

CONTENTS

Foreword 13

Preface 15

Introduction 19

Chapter One   The Healing Process Begins 23

Chapter Two   Do You Know You Have Rights
                   to a Full Life? 33

Chapter Three   Dealing With the Stigma 41

Chapter Four   Be in the Right Place 49

Chapter Five   Caring for the Sick and Mentally Ill ..59

Chapter Six   Dealing With Fear and Anxiety 69

Chapter Seven   Saying the Right Thing 81

Chapter Eight   Celebrating Milestones 93

Chapter Nine   Sticking With the Word 101

Chapter Ten   Life Gets a New Meaning 111

Chapter Eleven   Taking Care of Our Bodies as
                   Temples of the Holy Spirit............121

Chapter Twelve   The End of the Road 129

Chapter Thirteen   The Importance of Testimonies 133

Chapter Fourteen   Eze's Story 143

                   Conclusion 149

                   Appendix A

Learning by the Word
Living by the Word
Yielding leading to direction
Active procurement
Of my Lord's gifting
Discovering
Cooperation with God
Is faith in Him
What you can see
Are often distractions
Focus on the unseen
Brings progression
Because the Creator
Lives in you!

By Eze Onah

FOREWORD

This is an extraordinary book which I personally would recommend for everyone. You don't have to be themed religious or be a born-again Christian to enjoy and get the message behind this book. It is a book that takes you through the walk of a wife and husband in their quest to beat an illness that has no human cure, through their faith and trust in the Lord.

In a world where most people put all their trust in the medical sciences and their current discoveries, a supposedly incurable illness becomes almost a death sentence, but this book gives everyone who reads it hope to fight on. Once I started reading it, I could not put it down. It is a love story, a faith story, a message, a biography, a history lesson, a true story, all put in one. You will read it and laugh, cry, and sometimes get angry, but one sure thing is that by the end of the story, your faith will be built up. If you are going through the same thing, you will suddenly start to see light at the end of the tunnel.

I happen to be the pastor to the couple in the story, and reading what they went through and how I was there to be of some help brought tears to my eyes. You just have to read the book; it is quite extraordinary.

Defying the Odds is a book I will highly recommend for everyone in a congregation, from the senior pastor down to the new convert. Everyone will be able to take something tangible away to help them with the present situation or even with someone they know.

The Bible tells us that there is nothing impossible with God. This book helps you to see this clearer. For indeed anything is possible; Eze's story proves this.

Pastor Nelson Ngoka
Pastor of Christ Embassy (Norwood Chapter, UK)

PREFACE

In writing any book on healing or on testimonies of healing, one is always very aware that many people, even Christians, argue tenaciously as to whether God still heals today or if He heals at will. Many Christians frequently pray without believing that they will receive answers. In fact, some don't even expect answers. Perhaps they feel disappointed from an experience in the past when prayers remained unanswered. When the answers come, some dismiss these answers, believing instead that "it is too good to be true." But nothing is too good to be true with God. Then there are others who doubt the authenticity of testimonies they hear and attribute healing to coincidences or may even try to explain these testimonies away.

This book has not been written with the intention to try and convince you on any of the points raised above. That is not my job or mandate. However, the words in this book have the ability to let you see for yourself that faith in God is contagious. What do I mean? *This book has the ability to stir your faith for you to receive that miracle you require!* This book is not based on heretics, neither is it an account of self-healing. This book is solely about the power, supremacy, and compassion of God. God's power heals and, more importantly, keeps you healed.

What gives me the audacity to write such a book? Close friends and family saw the steps my husband and I took toward winning our fight of faith and exercising our rights in Christ to a divine health. Jesus came to give us life to the full (see John 10:10). Some of our friends even had eye-witness accounts, tasting the realities of mental sickness or its effects. I am sure many may have resigned my husband to a life of medication and recurrent bouts of mental sickness, and who could blame them? The odds were stacked against him. I do not by any account today make light of our journey, however. A journey in which there were times I cried to God in apparent distress. I have wiped the tears just like many of you reading this book right now. During those times all I hoped for was an end to the torture of mental illness. A few times, I even felt like running away. But in the end, I came to realize it was faith, not my tears, needed to get the victory we so immensely and sometimes desperately desired. This is what gives me the audacity to write this book.

Often doctors can offer no permanent cure for mental illness, as with several other illnesses in the world today. My husband was on various medications for about sixteen years and was eventually discharged indefinitely in the eighteenth year. My husband can do much more today than he did before those eighteen years, before it all started. When doctors told my husband he must stay on medication that made him feel dopey and slowed him down, amongst many other horrible side effects, God had a better solution. I want to share that solution with you. This is what gives me the audacity to write this book.

Make no mistake, the devil tried to withstand my husband and I many, many times in various ways. This book gives an outspoken account of some of the setbacks we encountered. We can tell you frankly that we have also been there when the furnace seemed seven times hotter. How did we come out of the fire like those Hebrew boys in the Bible? I'll tell you how. The fourth Man was with us (see Dan. 3:25). I am stirred in my spirit to let people know that God is real, that the devil is a liar. This is what gives me the audacity to write this book.

I'll also be sharing how you can not only get healed but stay healed. My husband shares his own firsthand experience in the last chapter in this book. In this book, you'll find several biblical references, biblical stories, and lots of revelations on the subject of healing in conjunction with our own healing account. The Holy Spirit taught me a wealth of truths in His Word along the way in our journey. It is therefore practically impossible for me to stay silent about divine healing. My husband and I have witnessed the power of God. We have tasted it. This is what gives me the audacity to write this book.

I believe this book will enrich and empower you. One cannot write a book such as this without being equally enriched themselves. I told my pastor in writing this book that the Holy Spirit dictated to me what to write. One day, I got up and that nudging inspired me to sit in front of the computer and away my fingers went, hours on end. My first draft was written in about four weeks.

Yes, this book has taught me a lot of things along the way. It has even strengthened my own faith. It has given me the audacity to step out in faith and lay hands on the sick and very sick. And yes, they have recovered.

This book is for everyone, not just those diagnosed with mental illness and their families or carers—those who take care of them. Anyone can read this book. In fact, I wrote this book for the whole world. As you read, do so with an open heart. Put away any preconceived ideas. Let the words minister to your spirit and bring healing to your soul and body. I believe God will begin to speak into your heart as you journey through this book. Read this book expecting to receive something. Don't stop till you get to the end. Ignore the lies of the enemy. Remember, you already have been declared the victory in whatever situation or circumstance you are facing right now!

This is your day, your season to receive your miracle.

Stay blessed.

Zoe A. Onah

INTRODUCTION

It had been a long walk. Perhaps a marathon, even. How else then could one describe eighteen long years in the mental health care system?

But now it was all over.

"What am I going to do with you?" the consultant psychiatrist asked my husband, Eze. For a moment, no one said anything.

Eze and I had the Master Physician's report engrafted in our minds. The report said that Eze was whole according to the Word of God. Would the consultant's report now line up with the Master's?

"I am discharging you indefinitely," the consultant finally said.

It took every self will in me not to jump over the consultant's table to hug the consultant. It took every self will in me not to yell or scream. I was more than excited. A day everyone had prayed for had finally arrived. This meant no more consultation visits, no more prescribed medication. Boy, I remember three years prior to this, one of the doctors giving Eze a stern warning never to come off the medication, ever!

"Good luck. I hope not to see you again, but if you do need help...."

But if you do need help...?

A switch went off somewhere in the recesses of my mind. I certainly was not interested in hearing what we needed to do in the event of uncertain so-called eventualities. I knew for certain that we would never need anything from the world of psychiatric medicine again. But what gave me this boldness?

Don't get me wrong. Eze and I have immense respect for the field of medicine. We certainly know that God uses doctors to demonstrate His healing power. Who else has given doctors their wisdom but God? But when doctors had insisted Eze stay on drugs indefinitely in their attempt to keep the sickness under control, we had tried to resist this life sentence with every fiber of our being.

Several knockbacks later, we had finally come to the end of the road. Along the way, we had learned to rely on nothing but the Word to get out of hazardous pits, each pit deeper and darker than the last.

But thank God for the Word of God! The Word had been what had got us this far. No one needed to tell us that for Eze to stay out of this horrible sickness permanently, it meant continuing to apply the Word of God always. Applying the Word that said, "No one living in Zion will say, 'I am ill'" (Isa. 33:24). One thing was for sure, no sickness was ever going to fasten itself to our bodies again!

The consultant was smiling now. The menu order was certainly smiles all around in the office. I imagined the jubilation going on with the angels in Heaven at that moment. A child of God, Eze, had put the devil to shame by walking away from sickness.

"Doctor, it was nice meeting you, but we sure don't want to see you again!" I chipped in light-heartedly, though meaning every word. Eze nodded his head in agreement, his every tooth on full display.

And we certainly don't need luck, good or otherwise!

Luck had played no part in getting us to the end of this journey. Instead of luck, we had an abundance of His grace (see Rom. 5:17). No Christian needs luck.

My husband put his arms around me as we waved our goodbyes. I tried to imagine the traffic activity going on in his brain. Eighteen years had been full of diagnoses ranging from depression to the final diagnosis of schizophrenia. Eighteen years had consisted of hospital admissions, outpatient treatments, medications up to his eyeballs, horrible side effects, and every trick and nook the enemy could throw in.

Like the woman with the issue of blood who had suffered for twelve years, we too had got hold of the Master's garment and in so doing appropriated healing (see Luke 8:43-48). The woman with the issue of blood had dared to believe in her healing. This was our testimony too. Faith had brought us this far, and faith was all we needed to go further.

God is Truth; satan is the liar. God's Word is truth. Oh, Eze and I had come to know the familiar taste of God's medicine. The Word had been Eze's medicine. Several times we had heard the Word preached that showed us that Eze was healed by the stripes of Jesus. Healing and divine health were officially our rights.

Yes, there was no denying those moments when Eze certainly did not *feel* he was healed. Yes, there was no denying those moments when Eze certainly did not *look* healed.

But we had had to take God at His Word and believe Him wholeheartedly. We knew certainly the victory had been won by Jesus. When Jesus died, He dealt with every sickness at Calvary. And every sickness included this monster, schizophrenia. This meant taking a stand not to be satan's ping-pong ball, batted about at will. The precious Blood meant we could be free.

My husband and I went through a process as we yielded to the Holy Spirit and allowed Him to direct our lives. Little by little, everyone started noticing the changes in Eze. God's Word was taking effect. God's medicine was healing Eze's mind.

A journey begins with a single step. That is all it takes. Never give up! The road may seem hard at times, but don't stop. If you get tired, catch your breath if you must, but resume where you left off. It is important you don't stop till you get to your destination. The destination with the sign-post of "healing and divine health." Remember, the enemy is under your feet no matter how hard he tries to *fool* you that he is supposedly strong. He was rendered powerless, but you've got to believe that. "And having disarmed the powers and authorities, He made a public spectacle of them, triumphing over them by the cross" (Col. 2:15).

The Word works!

You intended to harm me, but God intended it for good
to accomplish what is now being done, the saving of many lives
(Genesis 50:20).

THE HEALING PROCESS BEGINS

Winston Churchill was once famously quoted as saying that if one was going through hell, then one was to keep going. That sounds easier said than done.

For many in today's uncertain world, a living hell is real. Right here on earth. Many are coping or trying to cope with one trauma or another. Economic turmoil, raging health issues, and various threats of varying degrees, to name a select few, are some of the day-to-day issues many of us will face, are facing, or have faced at one time or another in our lives. One just has to tune in to the news broadcasts that hit our airwaves like bullets out of a canon and it won't take you long to conclude that the world we live in is in a lot of trouble.

Young and old, rich and poor, problems—or "challenges," the word I often prefer to use—affect everyone. Someone somewhere right now is either receiving news they'd rather not hear or they are right in the center of a new crisis.

But is life all that bad? Is this the abundant life that God promised us in His Word (see John 10:10)? When "less" is added to "hope," the result is hopeless. Too many people are doing less because of their challenges instead of having any hope at all. Where does one get the strength to get through another day of so-called bad news and the struggles in life?

Giving up is certainly not the answer. But many are at that point in their lives. Many have even made vain attempts at taking their lives. Even so-called worldly celebrities are no exception. In some societies, we hear of kids committing suicides. And these are not kids from some depraved part of the world.

The real hell by biblical accounts is a rough place. The real hell is not somewhere that civilized people would wish to spend eternity. Weeping and gnashing of teeth come as part of the menu. Torment is also part of the *carte du jour*. And, as if all that is not enough, hell has fire brewing.

But this is how life feels to some people who are very much alive. The fire rages cruelly, coming fast against them. And fire is violent. It is urgent. Fire moves quickly. Yes, even a five-year-old knows not to play with fire. To go through hell on earth is certainly no leisure trot in the park. Certainly, no time to hang about. Either that or you risk getting devoured by the flames. So we thank Mr. Churchill for his comment. It only makes sense to keep moving. But many don't.

God promised in His Word:

> ... *When you walk through the fire, you will not be burned; the flames will not set you ablaze* (Isaiah 43:2).

Right there in God's Word we can see that God does not want the flames of any fire to consume you. He does not even want you burned! You were not created to be an ash pile. No, leave that for the coals in your barbecue. You see those challenges you are facing right now are not designed to swallow you up!

What Is a Challenge?

Make no mistake; challenges will come even to the most faithful Christians among us. But before we go further, how do you define challenges?

Challenges, especially for a Christian, are things, circumstances, or situations that challenge our faith. Challenges are not designed to defeat a Christian. Remember, the Word has already declared that you are more than a conqueror (see Rom. 8:37). And that does not exclude the one faced with an apparently hopeless situation.

"More than a conqueror" means that we have gone past the conquering stage. We are now rejoicing and enjoying the spoils. We are now at rest in God, in that triumphant place where we are living in the victory of Christ.

Perhaps you have got to the stage where you are even asking, "Where is God right now in this challenge?" I'll tell you where God is. He is right there with you. Right there in the fire. God said He would never leave you nor forsake you. (See Hebrews 13:5 and also His promise to the Israelites in Genesis 28:15.) God wants to do something beautiful in your life even with that challenge that seems to hang over you like a dark cloud. The difference between charcoal and diamond is pressure. Which would you rather be?

You see, a challenge will either make you bigger and better or weaker and bitter. Which choice will you make? Challenges are meant for your promotion. They are springboards to a better life. Yes, I know, it does not feel like it when we are right in the center of one, but a challenge often signals a change for the better, especially for the Christian.

Challenges often take us out of our comfort zone. The temperature in the furnace is usually just hot enough to cause that shift we need but never too hot to smolder us. Always remember that, no matter how gigantic the challenge looks.

Challenges can be used to the best of our advantage. You'll discover how as you leaf through this book. But in the meantime you've got to keep moving. Keep going. Yes, to keep going through that hell experience means that you can't afford to give up, even now.

And that's why you are reading this book.

The Challenge of Mental Illness

Talk to anyone about mental illness and closely watch their response. Even if their words do not give them away in what they are thinking, I can assure you that their expressions will.

Mental illness is something that society scorns. Let's be honest, mental illness is something many even laugh at. Many carelessly use terms such as schizophrenics, mad people, or "nutters" in their jokes. But no one makes a joke out of someone with cancer. So why the difference?

Often this is borne out of ignorance of the disease or condition. Perhaps there is a tendency for people to see those suffering from other diseases as heroic and brave while those suffering from mental illness as wimps and weaklings. Yet everyone will know someone or of someone who has suffered one condition or another with regard to mental illness.

There are many good charities and medical staff who work tirelessly to ease the shame and pain of those who suffer from mental illness. They work hard to improve people's attitudes, combat discrimination in the workplace, and support carers. Yet in all their efforts, there are few if any long-lasting solutions or permanent cures. No promise of a permanent solution! Often the mentally ill are groomed to manage their symptoms in order that they can live some basic life at best.

A Promised, Better Life

But that is not God's agenda. You see, it is God who has the promise of that permanent solution which you seek. I like the New Living Translation's take on John 10:10: "…My purpose is to give them a rich and satisfying life."

Managing symptoms and spending half your life partially comatose because of drugs is by no means a rich and satisfying life. Such a life does not give glory to God whichever way you try and look at or explain it. Don't make excuses for God. He is God, after all. If God has promised something in His Word, then it must be so. If it is not, then don't try and explain it away by your experiences. Don't try to interpret the Bible by your experiences. Instead, let the Bible influence your experience.

You see, if Jesus never lived this kind of life, why should anyone? I can't find a single recorded account in the Bible where Jesus was ever sick physically, emotionally, or mentally! And if the Word of God tells me, "As He is, so are we in this world," then that means I am like my Father, God (1 John 4:17 NKJV). And where am I like Him? The end of that verse above says, "…in this world." That means right here on earth I am meant to be like Jesus.

Take this from me—nothing is too good for a child of God. You have been called to live the above and beyond measure life. That is what John 10:10 talks about. But there'll be time to delve deeper into this later.

Eze, my husband, had been through a battering of diagnoses of mental illness by the time I met him. After eighteen years, he was finally a free man, so to speak. Getting the discharge from the consultant psychiatrist was an unreachable dream that had finally been reached, but only through God's power and grace. Hear me—this was not a case of being discharged by the consultant psychiatrist with a "go home and as long you keep taking the drugs, you'll be fine" situation.

No! This was a sparkling clean bill of health from a consultant. I will never forget the look of, should I say, amazement in the consultant's eyes as he looked on as Eze and I embraced our news. In my quiet moments, I have often wondered what the consultant must have thought. But when God steps into any situation and rectifies it, men will wonder.

Eze had been through a range of diagnoses over the preceding years. The final diagnosis had been schizophrenia. What a sentence! But this consultant psychiatrist, who undoubtedly had several years' experience in his field, was now saying he even now disagreed with that original diagnosis. In other words, he was kind of implying that my Eze had been misdiagnosed.

Isn't God wonderful? When God heals, He certainly makes one whole. God can even go back into the past and wipe out those old horrible records. He makes the slate clean. God is neat. He does not do things by halves. That is my God. That is your God, our God!

Throughout this book, you'll read more of the challenges faced with mental illness. You'll find that no matter what the odds are that are stacked against you, God has not said no, unless of course *you* say no!

Forgetting the Pain of the Past

When I first met my would-be husband on an arranged blind date, as I sat opposite him at the restaurant looking into his big, soft eyes, I knew this was a very special man. A lovely persona originated around him. He was immediately likeable. He was no fashion icon, but I imagined him to have been strikingly handsome in his youth.

I could see that his eyes had a story to tell. I was not sure what this story was, but I sensed there were some sad twists and turns. Life had given him a few knocks. I could tell from his demeanor instantly. Besides, the mutual friend who had introduced us had given me a heads-up about "issues" Eze had. She had not gone into much detail but had told me it was vital I knew what they were. I had no idea how complicated or not these issues might be, so I felt guarded.

Eze's posture lacked confidence. His smile seemed incomplete. He perked his head to one side at an angle. His words sounded almost un-certain at times. Now and again he twiddled his thumbs. He spoke more of a glorious youth he had lived. Every other sentence started with "I used to be...." I began wishing I had met him all those years back, when he sounded like he had been ruling the world. I was getting a picture of a handsome genius who had been way ahead of his peers until something happened. I was not quite sure if I wanted to know what this something was. But I could see Eze seemed caught up in a glorious past. Was he afraid to let go of the past? Did the future look daunting?

The children of Israel had been through some traumas. A harsh Pharaoh was now ruler over them, and he showed no mercy. Their backs were familiar to the crack of the whips of the Egyptians. Pharaoh ceased to provide straw for them, doubling their labor.

But the Lord God of Israel heard their cries and came to their rescue. God had a glorious future for them. He had not forgotten them. He had made promises to their forefathers. His Word is yes and amen. His Word is the truth. That word spoken would surely come to pass in due season.

Isn't God so merciful? He hears our every cry like a mother to her baby. Enter Moses, God's extended hand. The deliverer sent to rescue the children from a wicked tyrant. One night they were free. While the Egyptian wailed, the Israelites rejoiced. God had come through for them.

However, the Israelites were short-sighted.

At the first sign of trouble, the Israelites soon began to remember the onions, leeks, and garlic they had eaten in Egypt. They murmured; they complained. They gave Moses hell! They looked back!

This story in the Bible is absolutely amazing. I can imagine that the Israelites only got to enjoy the luxuries of leeks and so on a very small fraction of the time compared to the hard labor they had to endure. Yet they craved for the old lifestyle.

To enter into the glorious future that God has promised all His chil-dren means taking a bold step. It means not looking back at the past whether good, bad, or both. "...Forgetting the past and looking forward to what lies ahead" (Phil. 3:13 NLT). In this Scripture, Paul was talking about forgetting his past in order to move ahead.

Paul had quite a few things I am sure he wanted to forget. Chief persecutor of the early Christians, he had a lot of blood on his hands. He had overseen the execution of Stephen, the first Christian martyr. But he also had some good things he had achieved. He was taking the Gospel of Jesus to the Gentiles. In spite of his shady past and the wonderful things he was doing at the time he wrote that to the Philippians, he spoke of straining toward what was ahead (see Phil. 3:13).

Eze had been the forerunner in his class at school. Though the youngest in his year, he was the brightest by far. A prodigy in many areas, he had many trophies of achievement. His teachers and friends alike knew that his would be a very bright future. But sickness had struck and slowed or even halted Eze in his tracks. He felt he could not create any new memories with a "record" such as his. Eze was now imprisoned by his past. It was safer living in a world that used to exist than the current brutal one he was currently living in.

Someone once said if you hold the past and present with both hands, you have no hand free to embrace the future. I like that. And it is so true. Another favorite quotation I have heard is this: "You can't drive safely if you are always looking at the rearview mirror instead of the windshield."

You may have had a wonderful life before trouble struck. Or you had a distressing past you'd rather not go into. Either way, God wants you to move on. You have to come out of Egypt. But it does not just stop there.

God always takes you out of something to bring you in. For example, He takes us out of darkness to bring us into His marvelous light. He took the children out of Egypt to bring them into their Promised Land.

Move into the promises that God has for you. With Eze, it did not happen overnight. It was a process. I like what the Lord promised in the Scripture below for the Israelites.

> *The Lord your God will drive those nations out ahead of you little by little. You will not clear them away all at once, otherwise the wild animals would multiply too quickly for you* (Deuteronomy 7:22 NLT).

Little by little is not a curse! God did not want the nations cleared out all at once. He needed them around to deal with the wild animals, or else the Israelites would have been faced with another problem, probably much worse than the enemies they had to contend with.

Allow God to work in your life. Do not get ahead of His plans and purposes for you. Walk with Him in the plans He has for you. Trust His plans. Yes, we are living in a microwave society now, where we want our dinners ready in five minutes and to be half way around the world in a few hours. There are times when supernatural speed will work in your favor, delivering things to you in record times. But when things don't happen overnight as we wish, don't throw in the towel.

A king does not give his prince a palace to run when he is five years old. You do not give your ten-year-old your car to drive, do you? *Do you?* Why? Because he or she has not reached the level of maturity that such responsibilities require. To give young children things at an early age might precipitate them into a path of destruction.

God is the same with His children. We may not get everything we need overnight just because we prayed. But if we walk with Him, we are sure to get there. The part we need to play is to continue to develop our faith, develop the knowledge we have of Him, and prove that we are maturing in the things of God. You may choose not to give your eighteen-year-old your car to drive yet because you may feel he has not shown you that he is capable of driving carefully. Until such time as he can prove himself, the keys are withheld from him (or her), right?

With love, I gently pointed out to Eze that he seemed to be stuck in the past. While I was intrigued to find out more about his history in getting to know him, he needed to *strain toward* what lay ahead. Talking incessantly about the life he used to live would never bring back those years. And his future as a Christian certainly did not depend on anything good or bad that had happened in the past.

> *Give no thought to the things which are past; let the early times go out of your minds* (Isaiah 43:18 BBE).

Isaiah, in the verse above, was telling the Israelites to forget about coming out of Egypt. This was one of the most important or significant parts of history for the Israelites. I wonder how popular Isaiah would have been after he said that! But Isaiah did not leave them without words of hope.

See, I am doing a new thing; now it is starting; will you not take note of it? I will even make a way in the waste land, and rivers in the dry country (Isaiah 43:19 BBE).

This is truly a verse of hope. It is a verse that will bring you hope to build your faith, no matter how hopeless you think your case is right now. This verse shows us there is a way out from whatever circumstances we are facing right now. God is able to put roads in the desert and streams in thirsty lands (see Isa. 43:19 CEV).

So are you prepared to let go? Decide today that the past is gone forever. Don't grope in the dark with memories of the past. If you keep doing the things you are doing now, you will keep getting the same results. To affect a change in your circumstances, you need to take a stand to change things.

It's a new order! God is more than able to do something new in our lives. Come out so that you may go in. Be bold and take a step. It may seem like a little step, but it is a step closer to victory. And God will do something new in you *today!*

Closing Thoughts

God is a good God. Perhaps you already know that Christians are not exempt from challenges. Jesus warned us, "I have told you these things, so that in Me you may have peace. In this world you will have trouble. But take heart! I have overcome the world" (John 16:33). This tells us that we have hope even in the midst of our troubles. But hear this. Jesus said these words before He had even died. With the finished work of the Cross which we enjoy today, remember, we established that we are also now more than conquerors. First John also tells us:

For everyone born of God overcomes the world. This is the victory that has overcome the world, even our faith (1 John 5:4).

No matter how big the challenge, it can never be bigger than Jesus dying for you. Instead of being concerned about the fire of your challenges, fan the flames of the fire of the Holy Ghost instead. The Holy Ghost is God in you. Depend on God and that fire will never go down.

It is important we remember the words quoted in the Scriptures above, especially when the thermostat of the fire temperature is turned up. When we look further into God's Word, you will find that God did not promise that there would be no "weapons." He did not promise either that the weapons may only be small ones. He said nothing about size, thrust, or strength. However, God said that those weapons fashioned against us would not prosper (see Isa. 54:17). Whether bow and arrow or weapons of mass destruction, none of these shall prosper. Praise God!

Summary

1. Challenges are circumstances or situations that challenge our faith.

2. Challenges are not designed to defeat a Christian.

3. A challenge will either make you bigger and better or weaker and bitter.

4. Managing symptoms and spending half your life partially comatose because of drugs is by no means a rich and satisfying life.

5. God can even go back into your past and wipe out those old horrible records. He makes the slate clean.

6. To enter into the glorious future that God has promised all His children means taking a bold step. It means not looking back at the past, whether good, bad, or both.

7. If you keep doing the things you are doing now, you will keep getting the same results. To affect a change in your circumstances, you need to take a stand to change things.

Confession

I refuse to give up. I am born of God. Therefore, I have overcome this world. I am a victor. I am more than a conqueror. I am triumphant in every situation. I have closed the door to my past. Every setback is a setup for my comeback. I am pressing forward instead to the life that God has for me. In Jesus' name, amen.

Do You Know You Have Rights to a Full Life?

Don't Manage Those Symptoms

There are many people around the world who have one incurable disease or another. An incurable disease does not necessarily equate to a terminal disease. And often, because some of these diseases are not terminal, people put up with the symptoms; they are quite content even to tolerate the sickness. They "manage" the symptoms. For example, someone suffering from migraine headaches may have devised a plan to cut out cheese completely from their diet, even though cheese is something he or she enjoys eating very much. But they know that if they take one single piece of pizza, the next three days will be torture. But make no mistake. Before long, there is a whole range of things that have been cut off from the diet. Is that the best quality of life God can offer you?

Managing symptoms comes in varying degrees. There are those who even have to manage pain. They go to pain management sessions where they are taught how to live with their agonizing ordeal. The pain cannot be eradicated, so strategies are devised. What a life!

The fact is that you can say *no!* The fact is that you can make your mind up that you have had enough. You can determine that you wish to have a better quality life than the one you are putting up with right now.

No Incurable Disease With God

Before I go much further, let me start by first asking: What is your definition of an incurable disease? My simple definition is this. No disease is incurable in the strictest sense of the word. I will pause for a minute while that registers in your brain!

Shocked? OK, let us examine this simple fact.

There are many diseases in the world today that are very easily cured, yet if we were to go back a few decades, they were once life-threatening conditions with no hope at all. Tuberculosis (TB) is one such disease. Once deemed an "incurable disease," today TB is easily treatable. How did that happen? Man found the right drugs for it. There was a remedy for TB even when people were helplessly dying as flies from it. But the snag was no one knew what that remedy was. Then one fine day came, someone found the cure, and the rest is history. All it took was someone to find the solution.

Likewise, in many parts of Africa, malaria was once a dreaded disease. Today, this is no longer the case with not just curative drugs but even preventative ones too. The same can be said for many diseases today.

A disease is therefore termed incurable as long as humans have found no cure for it. However, the reality is that there is a cure for HIV and cancer. The fact is that we have not found it yet. OK, let me explain that further. The fact that I have not found my diamond stud earrings that fell through the back of my sofa does not mean that the earrings do not exist, does it? Even if those earrings eventually end up in some landfill site, the earrings still exist. It's just that I can't find them!

So in the natural we are limited by the wisdom of the science and medicine world. I applaud the scientists who work to bring solutions; and as we come to the end of the age, there will be many scientific breakthroughs in many things, including the field of medicine. However, there are many breakthroughs in science that are still years away. And when you consider the new diseases that are being discovered as well all the time—one year bird flu, the next swine flu, and goodness knows what next—do we just coast along accepting anything that comes along?

We often determine the severity of the news we receive from our doctor based on the latest developments for a cure of the disease. A doctor diagnosing you with a headache will conjure a different reaction from a doctor diagnosing a stroke. Am I right?

Yet besides all these facts, God is in a class of His own. The Creator and Maker of humankind, God has the answers to even incurable diseases. It means that *anything is possible with God.* So that means if we find ourselves in a situation where everyone is shaking their heads sympathetically at you, it is time to put away those tissues and stop crying. For God has a way out. All it requires is your faith passport and trust ticket in God to change that hopeless situation.

God's way will lead you out of that life of bondage of pain and trauma into a better life of peace and joy. It is not time to start gathering everyone around to say your last goodbyes and tidying up the affairs of your life. Not if you are not ready to die yet. God needs you. Yes, it may shock you, but He does. He needs you here on earth, and if dead you can't accomplish much.

Yes, you need to flex those faith muscles and get out of your pajamas, pull those curtains open and get ready to live. For God wants you to live in spite of your prognosis. God wants you to keep going in spite of those debts almost forcing you onto the streets. You must exercise your right to live. And live well too!

The Right to Live

Shortly after I met Eze, it became apparent to me that he did not seem to have much of a prayer life. He never missed church; in fact he attended two churches every Sunday, back to back.

There was no doubt in my mind that this was a man who loved God. He had grown up in a Christian family where Bible study and prayer had been the order of the day. All his immediate family, including his parents and siblings, were born-again Christians. The first time I spoke to his mother, I could sense the burning passion this lady had for the things of God. In fact, she told me she was happy her son had met a Christian lady. It had been her prayer, and there was no compromising on that score where her approval lay.

When I questioned Eze as to what his prayer life was like, he responded that he did not pray much or even at all as he did not have anything to pray about! It took me more than a few minutes to compose myself from the shock of his response. It was not what I had been expected. I imagined him to be praying incessantly, even if he was praying amiss.

By this time, I had a brief picture of his medical history. Fourteen years beforehand, on a planned holiday trip abroad to see his parents in the country in which they lived, his life suddenly took a 360-degree twist. Collapsing at the airport, Eze woke up to find himself in a strange environment. Although he was not in total awareness, he could ascertain that this was a hospital of sorts. He was later to find out that this was a mental hospital.

Not many days later, his mother traveled urgently to see her beloved son, her firstborn son, who was now very ill.

As you can imagine the anguish of any mother, many thoughts must have shot through her mind when she saw her son. This was not the son she had reared. He did not belong to this place, this hospital, this institution! The medical staff was pumping into him all manner of drugs. Being a nurse herself, she knew the potency of these drugs. Some of these drugs could be highly addictive. She wanted him off them immediately.

The diagnosis came. Eze was suffering from depression. There had to be some mistake somewhere. Eze? Her bright son, the one who had studied civil engineering, was now mentally ill according to the doctors. Could life be this cruel?

Eze was later told that the depression he had been diagnosed with was "hypnotic" depression. It is quite possible he may not have heard this correctly, as in writing this book I have been unable to find such a medical reference. More likely, it is quite possible his diagnosis was psychotic depression. His symptoms included hallucinations without the aid of hallucinogens, a loss of reality, and feelings of intense pain, which were probably psychological. Over the course of the years, as Eze was diagnosed with mental illness, those were the recurrent symptoms. His consciousness would be about what was going on in his waking memories, and he would not be aware of his surroundings. Interestingly, he could speak to people in response to what they were saying, but not remember the conversation or anything about the event afterward.

Eventually, Eze was discharged and brought home, released into the care of his pastor and eventually his mother, only on his mother's insistence. For two years, she stayed at his home, nursing him better while trusting in God to bring back the son who once was bursting with life and gusto.

"Fine" was her pet name for her son. But now, his fine looks looked perturbed and even contorted under the influence of drugs. Meanwhile back home, the rest of the family grieved in their heart for the awful sentence that a diagnosis such as mental sickness brings. His father had once had hopes for him. An engineer himself, he had an established engineering firm. It had been his dream that one day Eze would return to take over the business, a legacy he had established for his generations to come. He wondered if this dream would ever happen now.

Eze was off work for a year. This was no jet set recovery.

Fourteen years on, when I met Eze, even though he had recounted the events of this episode to me, I knew much work was yet to be done in order to win victory over the evil dark world of mental sickness. But I couldn't believe what I had just heard in answer to my question on his prayer life. With the phone glued to my ear, disbelieving, sitting there staring at some blank space on the wall, I found it hard to reconcile that Eze could think he had nothing to pray about.

"Well, the fact you are on medication to prevent you from getting ill seems like a good cause for you to be praying, don't you think?" I was intrigued.

"Yeah, you're right. I never considered that!"

The devil is the number one trickster. One of his main strategies is to blind people, and Christians are no exception. Many "nice" Christians are happy to go through life putting up with things they are clearly not happy about.

I once read an interesting true story from a preacher. A woman came up to him one day to ask for prayers. She was not feeling well, so she asked the preacher to pray for a particular sickness she was suffering from. The preacher prayed and she was healed immediately. As the lady walked away, the preacher noticed that she had a limp or something and called her to come back so he could pray for her. The lady retorted that she was fine with the limp, she could handle it. Her priority was to get rid of the one she could not handle and that need had been met!

What an amazing but sad account. I often wonder if as Christians we limit the extent of our prayers and expectations because we think God's hand is short. Many of us are prepared to live with a situation till eternity if need be, as long as we can "cope" with it.

Eze knew that as long as he took his medication faithfully, he could get by in life. Get by! No. No Christian must get by in life. We must take our stand.

This is why I love the meaning of my husband's name. *Eze* actually means "king." As Christians we must know we are kings! (See Revelation 5:10.) Kings reign and rule. Kings are definitely not beggarly. They do not get by. They know they have power and authority in their kingdom and will do everything within their remit to protect their kingdom.

A Christian who is beggarly is at a serious disadvantage. A Christian who thinks he or she has to negotiate or compromise with the devil is always going to be at satan's whim anytime the devil chooses to take him or her on a joyride. That Christian cannot live life to the full. Jesus said, "...I have come that they may *have life*, and have it to the *full*" (John 10:10).

A life of putting up with symptoms does not sound like a full life to me. This is one of the reasons why Jesus came, to give us this full life. Do you know that? Are you aware of that? Are you participating with that knowledge?

If Jesus came to give us this life, then this life must be our right.

I told Eze that he did not need a life of drugs. For one thing, these drugs were not free. They cost money. That money could be donated to the things of God in propagating the Gospel. Second, the drugs had side effects. Ugly side effects.

Given that people have a tendency to put on weight as they get older, I could see that Eze was having issues with keeping his weight under control. The drugs caused him to balloon. He was clearly very unhappy about his weight issues. In fact, it was one of those things that was on his list of "I used to"!

I was fully aware that every time he tried to stop taking the medication, in few weeks or months he would find himself back in the hospital, another piece of his dignity stripped from him. But the full life was his right. He needed to insist on those rights. He needed to determine that somewhere in the future it could and would happen. Faith would be the currency for this to happen. But it was certainly not impossible!

I loved and admired Eze's resolve. His determination was as strong as steel. He wanted to get rid of this horrible monster. His heart was open to godly counsel. The first battle had therefore been won.

Step by step, Eze was taking this journey. Obviously, by the time we got married we were in this together. "'And the two will become one flesh.' So they are no longer two, but one" (Mark 10:8). We could not see the road far ahead, but the Word was guiding us. The Word was a lamp to our feet and a light for our path (see Ps. 119:105). It was only illuminating each step.

In biblical days, lanterns were tied to the traveler's feet as they journeyed down paths in the darkness of the night. They would not be able to see way ahead of where they were going, but they could see one step at a time as they walked down the paths.

This was truly our story. We knew our destination was healing and health. We could not see it with our *physical* eyes, but with our rights in Christ firmly engraved in our hearts, we knew there was no giving up on getting to that destination!

Closing Thoughts

God has called us to live a full life. In fact, the word "life" is taken from the Greek word *zoe*. *Zoe* means the God-life. That is the life that is in God. That is the life that was imparted into your spirit when you became a Christian. What that means is that God has put that life in *you!* This is surely something to be excited about.

Zoe is the presence and nature of God. This *zoe* literally means life that is indestructible, incorruptible, and undefeatable. It is divinity supplanting humanity, not divinity alongside humanity. No, you don't have two natures. God is not confused to give you two natures. That is like saying God has given you two personalities!

So what is this divine nature? There is a bug going around in the office. What do you do? You reject its power over you. Will you be a victim of it? No, we have been made victors in everything, which includes resisting germs. It is up to you. You don't have to settle for the lower life of bugs and viruses anymore. Why? Because there is a higher life in Christ called *zoe* that gives you rights to enjoy more. Hey, I did not promise this. God did.

Yes, the *zoe* life is the God life, life-giver, absolute fullness of life. It is the king life. Kings exercise authority. They refuse the beggarly life no matter what! That is the way earthly kings are trained. How much are you?

Can you perceive how big this is? You need to spend some time meditating on this till it jumps in your spirit! It is a crying shame if you have to put up with chronic pain. Yes, a crying shame if you have to live with something uncomfortably uncomfortable all the days of your life! No, not when you have the divinity genotype flowing through your blood— the DNA of God. Unless you can see and walk with the consciousness that you are not ordinary, you will be subjected to anything that comes your way. You must carry the consciousness of this God-life.

Live with this consciousness of your divine origin. Before long, as you meditate on this consciousness, you will be living out the life in reality.

Summary

1. You can make your mind up that you have had enough of those symptoms. You can determine that you wish to have a better quality life than the one you are putting up with right now.

2. A disease is incurable as long as humans have found no cure for it.

3. There is no incurable disease with *God*.

4. Anything is possible with God.

5. A Christian who is beggarly is at a serious disadvantage. A Christian who thinks he or she has to negotiate or compromise with the devil is always going to be at satan's whim anytime the devil chooses to take him or her on a joyride. That Christian cannot live life to the full.

Confession

I know who I am and whose I am. I have the zoe life in me. I am not subject to the elements of this world. Therefore nothing gets me down. No sickness, no disease, no challenge. I choose to live life to the full. In Jesus' name, amen.

——————————————————————————

Chapter Three

DEALING WITH THE STIGMA

You Are Beautiful

When was the last time someone complimented you? Perhaps it has been an age. Perhaps you have never received a kind word in your entire life. However, do you know how beautiful you are?

You see, when God created man, we are told He saw it was *very* good (see Gen. 1:31). All the while God's commentary on His creation had been "good." Now God was even more impressed with His works. God sure liked what He saw.

I find it interesting how various illnesses and sicknesses raise eyebrows negatively. How certain categories of sickness become a stigma in society.

God never created anyone ugly. So often stigma tries to create an ugliness out of people or their situations. Yet God made human beings the crowning glory out of all His creation. Sickness was never part of God's plan and still isn't, because sickness scars and mars. That is why we must refuse sickness. In essence, we are too beautiful to be sick. We have been wonderfully and fearfully made (see Ps. 139:14).

If you have been wonderfully and fearfully made, how dare society take a poke at you? Do people know who you are? The Bible says we are kings (see Rev. 1:6). Yes, that is who you are. Whoever made mockery of a king? Do that in ancient times, and you could be executed!

It is imperative you see yourself as God's masterpiece. His prized possession. It does not matter who is laughing at you right now. People may call you all sorts of names. Maybe labels of things you are or have even been "guilty" of, such as a drunk or a prostitute. No, those labels are not there with you to stay. Those labels are not tattooed on your forehead. And so what if they were?

When you come to Jesus, He says:

> *Therefore if any man be in Christ, he is a new creature: old things are passed away; behold, all things are become new* (2 Corinthians 5:17 KJV).

The New Living Translation says, "The old life is gone; a new life has begun!" So why settle for anything less than the offer of a new life? Who cares what others have called you? All that matters is what God calls you. Jesus hung around with some of the scorns of the society, the tax collectors who were big cheats, the prostitutes, robbers, and so on. He did not purposely seek the crème of the society, the well-learned men, the Pharisees who were too far to see, and the Sadducees who were too sad to see!

All God says is that you are beautiful. You are blemish free.

Jesus Never Scorned Anyone

In biblical days, lepers were considered unclean. Lepers were one of the outcasts of society. To some extent, one might understand that with a disease as highly contagious as leprosy, it was safe to keep your distance for fear of catching the disease too. A horrible disease, leprosy often disfigured its victims. As if the disfigurement was not terrible enough, lepers wore certain clothes to distinguish themselves. They were kept in isolation from their families. I can also imagine how worthless, lonely, unloved, and abandoned they must have felt.

No one touched lepers, for if they did they were rendered unclean too. But one Man did. That man was Jesus. He loved even the lepers, the ones who had been stigmatized by society; the ones who everybody laughed at!

> *A man with leprosy came and knelt before Him and said, "Lord, if You are willing, You can make me clean." Jesus reached out His hand and touched the man. "I am willing," He said. "Be clean!" Immediately he was cured of his leprosy* (Matthew 8:2-3).

Jesus expressed his willingness to heal the leper. I like how the Bible in Basic English words Jesus' response: "It is My pleasure; be clean." Jesus was sure pleased to be of help. He did not come to heal certain types of sicknesses, the ones that were socially acceptable, perhaps the colds and coughs only. No, He made no distinction. He healed all manner of illness and disease when the sick were brought to Him (see Matt. 8:17).

In Matthew 8:3, we read that Jesus *touched* the leper. No one was allowed to do such a thing by the Law. But a loving Jesus did. He violated the Law on account of a show of love. He touched the leper as if it was the most natural thing for Him to do. Remember though, Jesus did not touch everyone whom He healed. He could have just spoken the word for the leper's healing.

Imagine how that touch must have felt for the leper. Who knows how long it had been since the last time he experienced the touch of another human being. It could have been months, perhaps years. The leper must have felt dehumanized. That touch from a caring Jesus reached an aching heart. It was the healing balm the leper needed. Jesus made him feel accepted, like a human being again. I am sure that day the leper received emotional healing apart from his physical healing.

There is power associated with a touch from God. Did you know that God even designed human beings so that when we touch people we care about there is a hormone that is produced? That hormone, informally called the love hormone or the cuddle hormone but known as oxytocin, calms, soothes, and heals. In fact, recently researchers at the University of California were studying whether the hormone released with touches and hugs can help patients diagnosed with schizophrenia.

No doubt, when I met Eze he did not have a lot of self-esteem. Though confident that he had not lost his many abilities and talents, he felt that this was relevant only if the past could be erased and he was healed completely. Some women he had met in the past had seemed to be uninterested.

I believe there were several reasons for this. They were looking at the person on the outside and the product of several years of battering in the mental health system. They were short-sighted and failed to see the unearthed potentials of the jewels and treasures inside the man. Those who showed any interest were merely interested in what they could get to take them out of possible penury or perhaps get their one-way ticket to the Western world.

The fear of losing anyone who showed any interest on account of his so-called medical history also brought fresh fears. The odds seemed stacked against him. Stigma had created its own fresh problems.

The manifestations of the works of the devil are the manifestations of his works whether someone has a cold or has HIV. Don't be fooled; the enemy's strategy is to kill, steal, and destroy (see John 10:10). That is why, as I said earlier, we must insist on our rights to live the full life. A cold soon develops into the flu and then on to something more serious.

The devil is merciless. He is wicked. Never settle for anything from him, no matter how small. That is why we must not bring ourselves down to a low level of pointing fingers at people who society thinks are the low-lifers and outcasts. *No!*

Don't classify the devil's work for him. They are *all* bad, very bad. Not one of them is good, because there is nothing good about him. Just because the devil has inflicted your body with a "leprosy" does not make you inferior to the person sporting a headache. They are all his works.

Stick your head high and let people know that yes, you may not feel or look fine now. But in a matter of time, just a twinkle of an eye, they will see for themselves that your situation has turned around.

Jesus is not afraid to touch you. He is not afraid to be in the same room as you. We have another touching example when Jesus healed the Gerasene demoniac. The full account can be read in Mark 5:1-20.

Here was a man who had lost his mind. He lived in tombs. His antisocial behavior had probably put him in such confinement. Imagine how cold and dark it is to live in a tomb, but this man had made such an environment his home. Many had tried to control this man with chains and fetters, but madness had given him incredible strength. He broke the chains apart. This was the Incredible Hulk of his day. He howled from those tombs like a hyena day and night, cutting himself with stones. Imagine his open sores. Imagine his torn clothes. People probably ran away from him if they saw him at a distance. This man was worse than a pit bull terrier off its lead!

Later in the story, we read how the man ran up to Jesus when he saw the Master. Jesus did not then take off in an Olympic hundred-meter dash. He dealt with the demons that were tormenting this man senseless.

What is even more beautiful about the story is that when he was healed, the ex-demoniac then went ahead and cleaned himself up, putting on clothes. (Remember, the people came and found him as such; I believe no one got the clothes for him.) For all to see, this man now had a sound mind. You could imagine everyone would be dancing and jumping all over the place. Oh, no. The Bible records they were afraid. The Contemporary English Version says they were terrified! There is no pleasing some people. They were scared of the demoniac when he was wild, and now he was healed they were still scared. What these people needed was to change their mentality.

Unfortunately, you can't go around trying to change what people think of you. People are entitled to believe what they choose. It is the basic right of every human being. Only the Word of God has the power to change the mindset of people. Only the Word of God can transform a person's mind and fill it with the right thoughts.

Share Your Testimony

That is why we must share our testimonies. As we share our testimonies, people begin to understand the power of God's Word and begin to realize the devil can never be on their side. Once people come to that realization, stigmas can be eradicated in their minds. We will look at the importance of testimonies later, especially with regard to keeping your healing and miracles.

In the meantime, rest in the knowledge and assurance that Jesus knows no stigma. Jesus wants to be involved in your life. He wants to bring a touch into your life. Jesus is not standing far away from you. In fact, if you are a Christian He lives right inside your heart. He is with you everywhere you go.

Eze told me later in one of our tête-à-têtes that he was happy to have found someone like me who could love him as a person. It sure helped him realize that he did not need to live under any further stigmas. He could stick his head up high as a king, because as Christians that is who we are (see Rev. 5:10).

Another right in Christ! Little by little. Another step to victory!

Closing Thoughts

You are made in the image and likeness of God (see Gen. 1:26). This shows how valuable you are to God. No matter what life has thrown at you, it means that God still sees you as His best. You are beautiful to God. Remember, He gave us His best—His Son on the Cross for us. Jesus suffered a terrible death for every person in the world. It was not in vain. How much do you price a man's blood, much more the Blood of Jesus? This means we are priceless.

See yourself as God sees you. Embrace the love and touch of Jesus. As you do, the sting of stigma and scorn becomes less painful. Concentrate on the light and not on the darkness. It will help you move forward. But one caution—don't move forward with bitterness in your heart to those who may have laughed at you. Trying to move forward with bitterness will instead take you backward. Jesus on the Cross prayed for forgiveness for those who spat at Him and shouted all forms of abuse. He loved them in spite of their mockery. That love has been shed abroad in your heart, and you too can extend love and in so doing liberate yourself from hurt and pain (see Rom. 5:5).

Remember always just how immensely blessed you are because He paid the price.

Summary

1. You have been wonderfully and fearfully made.

2. See yourself as God's masterpiece. He wants to display you.

3. Jesus made no distinction between those He healed. He knows no stigmas. He touched the leper, something that was forbidden to do.

4. Don't classify the devil's work for him. They are *all* bad. Not one of them is good, because there is nothing good about him.

Confession

I am the very best of God. I am beautiful, precious, and priceless. I am the apple of God's eye, special to God. It does not matter what others say I am. I know who I am. Thank You, Father, for paying the price for me. I am blessed. In Jesus' name, amen.

BE IN THE RIGHT PLACE

Position Yourself for Success

There are many definitions of success. My dictionary defines success as, "favorable outcome, attainment of an object, wealth, or fame, etc." There are many who have obtained favorable outcomes in a decision only to realize it was the wrong decision. Likewise, there are many who attain wealth and fame but die of some overdose or overindulgence. Many zoom in and out of rehab as if rehab has now become their bedroom.

So success cannot be defined by the definition above. God must have a better definition of success than this. Success is not a case of going up to come down. Joshua 1:8 (KJV) talks about *good* success. Therefore it means that there must be *bad* success.

So, what is important about success in a book like this? Our desire for the outcome of whatever we seek to achieve in life is always one of success. No one gets into a race to lose. No one wants to be branded a loser. Therefore, it is important we seek godly ways of how we can achieve good success in everything we do and in getting results and solutions to our challenges. We desire good outcomes, and that is what God desires for you too.

If we remember the story of Joseph in the Bible, even though he was a slave God still regarded him as a successful man. And because of this success, Joseph's life went from glory to glory till eventually he became a prime minister. This means that even in your challenge, even if you are in a minus position, you can still be a success. That success is your "get out of jail free" card! And one way of achieving good success is being in the right place. It is positioning yourself for success.

The Right Church

A lot of times, we put a lot of emphasis on choosing the right place to live, work, school our children, and so on. All these things are important decisions. Making poor choices in life can create inconveniences or even have negative consequences or a lasting impact.

I mentioned earlier that when I met Eze he was already attached to two churches. However, after we got married I suggested to him that it would be more practical to make a choice of worshiping at one instead of making a mad dash between the two every Sunday and hence not fully participating in either.

Where you worship and/or the ministry you belong to is vitally important for a Christian. This cannot be overemphasized. You need to be in the right place among the right people hearing the right things.

Eze soon realized that in order to be firmly grounded in the things of God, he would need to make a decision. That way he could give 100 percent of his attention to the assembly he belonged to. It is important to be in the right place in order to hear the right words that will ultimately mold your life.

The right church will always be a church where the Truth is preached. The right church is based on biblical principles. The right church is where God wants you to be so you can grow, be discipled, and be used as a tool for God. Some people often ask how they can know what God wants for them and their lives. How can they be in the center of God's will? The answer is simple. It is being in the right environment where you will discover and find God's perfect will. And that right environment is the church that God has planted you in.

Finding the right church is not about denominations or the description of the name of the church. It is not about where you have been since your mother carried you in her womb! It is not about size or numbers either. In fact, when Eze made his final decision we eventually went to a new branch that had been opened from one of the churches he had frequented. There were only a small number of about thirty congregants every Sunday!

But it was God's plan for us to be rooted there. God surely led us there. I must admit, having come from a larger congregation where the size of the choir was bigger than the congregants at my newfound church, I was slightly miffed. But the reality in hindsight was that I was missing my old environment and somehow like the children of Israel longed to go back. With adjusting to the newness of marital life, those early days seemed like a tall order!

But within my heart of hearts I knew that I had to stay. Never one to be a church hopper, I made up my mind to stick with it. This was confirmed by a nudging in my spirit that told me to stay put and not be moved by numbers. Our dear Friend the Holy Spirit, no doubt!

Why am I saying all this? Because commitment to a church is one of the key vital organs that keeps you alive spiritually. Some people shy away from commitment. They don't want accountability. Some prefer to be lost in a crowd. Some feel they are too busy to give their all to matters relating to God, or they don't know how to.

Submit to Godly Leadership

Our wonderful pastor was and is a true father to his congregation. He truly watches over his sheep. I must admit he played a large part in helping me feel welcome during those early days of uncertainty when my eyes kept looking toward the door to go back to my former spiritual house of worship.

But everyone desires their pastor to be truly a spiritual father. I truly believe our pastor has one of the kindest smiles on the planet. I am sure if you are in the right place too, you will say the same of your pastor. That smile was healing in itself. It was a special gift. It was the assurance I needed that everything was going to be all right.

Yes, you must have confidence in your pastor. He is the shepherd of your soul. God recognizes the authority a pastor has over you. God never bypasses authority. God used the voice of Eli when he called Samuel. Why? Because God realized that Samuel was under the care of Eli, and Eli had spiritual authority over him. Therefore Eli, being the shepherd over Samuel's soul, could hear from God in order to tell Samuel how he was to respond the next time God called.

Thank God that Eli allowed himself to be used by God in order to give Samuel the right advice.

So Eli told Samuel, "Go and lie down, and if He calls you, say, 'Speak, Lord, for Your servant is listening.'" So Samuel went and lay down in his place (1 Samuel 3:9).

The pastor that God has placed over you will give you the right advice. Why? Because one way God talks to you is through those in authority over you, especially your pastor. What would have been Samuel's destiny if Eli had just said to him something like, "Oh Samuel, you keep hearing voices; it's just your imagination. Go, lie down and don't come back here again!" Who knows if Samuel would have missed God's timing!

OK, you might be thinking, *Well, I think my pastor has given me the wrong advice.* Be 100 percent sure on this before going against your pastor's counsel. A safe barometer, for example, would be advice contrary to the Word of God. For example, if your pastor told you to marry someone else's husband!

Another point is that if you are 100 percent sure that the advice is contrary to the Word (remember you may not know everything), even if your pastor tells you to do something that you are not sure of, God can cover those mistakes and still make them work out for good for you. This is because God understands spiritual authority. He knows that you are submitting to those placed over you and will not let you suffer as a result of this.

So don't mess along the lines on how you revere your pastor. As I said, he is the shepherd of your soul, and having the right pastor means he would surely want the best for you. But you must trust that your pastor is hearing from God. And being in the right place is the first clue to that.

Samuel did as Eli had instructed him to do. He could have thought that the old man was senile and did not know what he was talking about. That may have caused Samuel to miss God's timing. Samuel had a part to play too.

Eze and I submitted to the authority of our pastor. So we began to confide in our pastor in the issues we were facing regarding Eze's medical condition. As time went on, our so-called defenses came down as we kept our pastor in the full picture of what was going on. He knew of any setbacks we had and rejoiced over every milestone and victory.

Be Relevant in Your Church

But being in the right place did not only entail submitting to our pastor. Through the profound teachings of the branch we were in and the ministry as a whole, we learned that our spiritual growth was vitally important.

You see, many people get healed from all sorts of diverse sicknesses throughout the Body of Christ. However, many times, many find that in no time they have lost their healing, some even feeling far worse than they were initially.

> *When an evil spirit comes out of a man, it goes through arid places seeking rest and does not find it. Then it says, "I will return to the house I left." When it arrives, it finds the house unoccupied, swept clean and put in order. Then it goes and takes with it seven other spirits more wicked than itself, and they go in and live there. And the final condition of that man is worse than the first…* (Matthew 12:43-45).

Eze appropriating his healing was one thing high on our agenda for sure. But there was no point in being healed for a month only to end up far worse later. I am sure you would not want to end up in a worse situation than you currently might be in after overcoming it a few weeks before, right?

Being in the right place also means positioning yourself to grow and be developed. Growth and development will help you to handle life's challenges when they come. The best place to learn new things and discover your talents is in the house of God. I am a testimony of that for sure.

I was one of those people who, unless asked, had no problem being a seat warmer every Sunday in church. Yes, I loved God and supposedly *all* the things of God, but you would not catch me volunteering to be a worker in the church.

Well, I got a shock of my life when on my second Sunday in my new church I was asked what I could do to help out!

Help out? I thought to myself, looking at the pastor's wife like she had suddenly landed from outer space. *I am still considering whether to stay or not!* My thoughts were all over the place.

Thank God she asked. I probably would not have got into writing much or even writing this book now if it had not been for my pastor's wife. Thank God she is persistent and insistent with the flock. Like a mother telling her child to do their homework because of the long-term benefits they stand to gain, so it was for Eze and me.

I told her I had some interest in writing, had done some in my last church, and could I look into doing newsletters for the church. She wholeheartedly embraced the idea and the rest, as they say, is history!

Eze, meanwhile, found himself in the deep end. A brother who used to handle the technical requirements of setting up the sound and video system was relocating, which meant he was leaving the branch. Eze was asked to step into the role. Eze had no idea what he was going to do or how he would manage such a big responsibility. He looked worried. If a microphone was not working from now on, he knew that all eyes would be on him. It seemed in the natural that the shoes of the leaving brother were not easy ones to fill.

But where else can one make mistakes and not get fired? The church.

As I had mentioned earlier, Eze did not have a lot of self-confidence when I met him. But God was now handing him the solution for this on a plate. Would Eze seize his moment of opportunity? Would he even recognize it?

Praise God, he did. Often times when we pray we think that the way God is going to answer is by shaking some magic wand somewhere in the heavens and hey, presto! The answer is staring us right in the face here on earth. For example, one minute Mr. Joe Blogs is concerned that he has no self-confidence; he prays, and the next second he is the most confident person in the entire planet!

Don't get me wrong—I know God does supernatural wonders. But often times our answers may not come in the way we expected. We need to be alert to know when opportunities arise that are in fact the answers to our prayers.

Eze seemed quite nervous the first Sunday he took over his new role. No doubt, he lived to tell the tale. He realized that no one was standing over him with a big stick if there were any slip-ups or technical difficulties. In fact, in those early days he was just a one-man band. When I could, I offered him a helping hand, but he did it all practically on his own.

Eventually the technical department grew in number and in requirements under his wing. He soon had about five people working alongside him. He was learning delegation; he was learning communication and taking responsibilities for other people's actions. The scope of work also increased as the church grew. Requirements for video recording, video editing, more sophisticated sound equipment and the like came onboard.

What was happening here? Eze's confidence started to grow. He began to see new abilities. He was slowly emerging from the shell he had hid himself in due to mental illness. Pastor held his work with high esteem too. Pastor knew this was vital in encouraging Eze. Eze's confidence started spilling over to his work in the office. His colleagues and a very understanding boss had till then covered for the work he often left undone. Mental illness had blinded his eyes not to even recognize that he was working under par and not working up to requirement.

But with the scales gradually coming off his eyes, he began to recognize that a change was needed in his work. He needed more confidence to get there. He needed to control the drowsiness the drugs were causing, but at least there was an awareness.

Being in the right place also meant being a pillar in the Body of Christ. Every child of God has been given gifts to build up the Body (see 1 Cor. 12:8-10). The gifts of the Holy Spirit are part of everything we need to find and fulfill our purpose and destiny in life. Jesus promised the Church that the works He did we would do, and also greater works too.

> *Verily, verily, I say unto you, He that believeth on Me, the works that I do shall he do also; and greater works than these shall he do; because I go unto My Father* (John 14:12 KJV).

How can we do what Jesus did and even greater things? Through the ability of the Spirit. The gifts are for equipping the Church. Where can you best discover your gifts and callings? In church and being in the right church, you'll quickly find them!

Before long, Eze and I began to see the operation of the gifts of the Holy Spirit in us. We began to see various gifts operating in us. We were confident we were in the center of God's will for our lives. Being in the right place, the right church was another step taken. Little by little we were getting there.

As we positioned ourselves as pillars in the Body of Christ, the layers of buildup of the disease were gradually coming off. And God's supernatural power was gradually becoming evident for every man and his dog in the world to see the changes in Eze's life and body.

We were winning. We were not "walking" to victory any longer. No, we were marching onward as soldiers of Christ. With our pastor and the church behind us giving their full support!

Closing Thoughts

If you need to catch a plane in Washington and instead you went to New York, I can assure you that you will not be on the right plane for your intended journey. Why do we ensure we go to Washington? Because we want to get to our destination.

God has made provision for us to get to our destination and He has told us where we are to be. He explicitly tells us, "Let us not give up meeting together, as some are in the habit of doing..." (Heb. 10:25). That is clear enough. God has a prescribed order. If we can follow a doctor's prescription by the letter because we trust that he has the knowledge to help us get better, it is a slap in the face of God if we think we have a better way than His prescription!

If we want God's help, then we must follow His ways. It is a choice. We each have a right to choose our way or God's way. But if we choose God's way and do as He says by regularly attending church, we will not be disappointed. There are some provisions and blessings God has made for us only *when* we assemble together. And those provisions cannot be accomplished anywhere else, much as we may try to compromise.

People who are depressed can find emotional healing by being of service in church. (We'll talk more about service in the church in a later chapter.) Usually when one is depressed, there is the likelihood to dwell on oneself or the circumstance or situation that may be contributing to or exacerbating the depression. Finding a purpose for your life certainly helps with feelings of worthlessness, hopelessness, or any negative feelings that depression brings along as allies. By helping out in church, you will have the opportunity to dwell less on the dark thoughts cramming your mind and instead refocus your energy on the project or task at hand. Service in the house of God turns your attention from your thoughts to others. It may be anything, like even helping to make coffee after service. Imagine the look of appreciation from the people you serve, the nod from the elderly lady who is grateful for something warm in her chest, and so on. If you had not had the opportunity to make that coffee, there would be no feeling of worth reciprocated. And the beauty at the end of the day is that any service in church will *always* yield something good. God steps in, angels come to your aid, and you always get a positive outcome. This may be the boost that depressed people need to snap out of their condition and pave the way to a permanent and lasting solution.

Summary

1. If we desire good success in all that we do, we must seek God's way first.

2. To be in the center of God's perfect will for your life means being in the right environment. The right environment is the church that God has planted you in.

3. When God wants to bless you, He will put you under the care of a man or woman of God.

4. Submit to the shepherd of your soul.

5. Your spiritual growth is important. This growth can be achieved by finding something to do in your church.

Confession

I am always in the right place. As I serve in my church, doors of blessings and opportunity are being opened to me right now. I will not give up on going to church, because God has not given up on me. I am success conscious. I am victory conscious. In Jesus' name, amen.

CARING FOR THE SICK
AND MENTALLY ILL

The Qualities of a Carer

There are millions of devoted people in the world who have given up many things in their lives just to look after their sick relatives or friends. A word of encouragement to you—God sees your efforts and they are not in vain.

Carers often need support themselves. Caring for the sick can be very draining, especially when done in your own effort. Trying to find the best solution and looking after the sick person while looking after yourself is really a full-time job. Carers can feel emotionally drained, among other things. They can feel like they need propping up too. Caring for the mentally ill comes with its own challenges. Dedication and courage are key attributes in this area, especially as the world of the mentally ill can often appear to be very daunting and unpredictable.

But God is your Rock and Strength in those moments of burnout and at all times too. If we can call on Him, He will surely give us the strength we need for another day. He will send help too. He will ease the burden. A carer who attends church—the right church, too as, we established in the last chapter—is in the best support group they could ever be in.

It is vital that carers maintain a positive attitude for the ones they care for. Largely, there are two classes of sick people, especially those who have been in their condition long enough. On one hand, you have the group who welcome help. This group is usually offended if help is not offered to them. The other group is fiercely independent as much as possible and do not wish to be "patronized" by your help and concern. However, with both groups, carers may often feel they will be walking on eggshells. With both groups, patience is the key. Lots and lots of patience. In fact when patience runs out, long-suffering should kick in!

A positive and patient attitude outside of God eventually leads to frustration and despondency when things do not seem to improve or your expectancy is not met. Or when those you are caring for do not seem to appreciate your efforts and sacrifice.

The solution for this can only be in being a carer with a difference. That is one who has the Spirit of God (and hence the fruit of the Spirit, including love and patience) and walks by faith and not sight (see 2 Cor. 5:7). Don't lose heart.

My Caring Experience

A few months before we got married, Eze made the decision to come off his medication permanently. I wholeheartedly agreed with him that it was the best decision to make. He hated the side effects. The weight gain, raised cholesterol, drowsiness, lack of concentration—the list went on and on.

Apart from that there were other physical ailments he got from time to time. In fact, it appeared to me that when he got off one, he went straight into another.

I knew his diet was not very healthy or balanced for starters. This I knew had its own contributory factors. I started going shopping with him, ensuring that he got his fruits and vegetables. I also encouraged him to drink a lot more fluids such as water. Every Sunday without fail, after church he came around for a hearty dinner. Sometimes, this was repeated in the week. I was and am also a firm advocate of having a good breakfast to start the day. I encouraged Eze that a good start would keep him alert and more productive.

His diet change was a practical solution. As Eze's diet improved, so did his health. Always check your diet and ensure you get enough rest too. As Christians, our bodies are the temple of the Holy Spirit (1 Cor. 3:16). If we look back at the Old Testament, the Temple of God was a holy and consecrated place. There were prescribed rules and regulations in ensuring the sacredness of this place where God resided. It is no different today. We must take steps to ensure we do not defile the Temple of

God through neglect, abuse, contamination, or even ignorance. As the salt of the earth, we must preserve our body by taking good care of it. One main benefit of doing so is that we keep healthy and keep a lot of "avoidable" diseases at bay. Jesus Himself ate a healthy Jewish diet that contained plenty of fish, whole-grain bread, legumes, and vegetables.

I also knew that some of the illnesses Eze faced back to back were of a spiritual nature, which meant that they were caused by an evil spirit. Jesus Himself healed many by casting out demons from the sick. Contrary to what many people may think or believe, the same is still true today. Over time, through various ministrations by our pastor, Eze became free from some of these recurrent illnesses and waved goodbye to them permanently.

For a few months after Eze came off his medication, his health was improving. He still had a way to go yet, but we celebrated the victory of the elimination from drugs in his life.

Then wham! I noticed one Sunday while talking to him on the phone that things just did not sound right. We later met up and I sensed things were amiss. I was concerned. I had no clue as to what form the illness took as I had never been party to witnessing this before. Anyhow, Sunday night I went to bed very worried. I spent the night praying the best way I knew how.

Monday morning after a fitful night, I decided instinctively to call him before heading off to work. When he answered the phone, my worst fears were confirmed. He was not making any sense at all. I needed to see with my own eyes, however.

Brushing my teeth and picking up the first clothes I could find, I ran to my car and literally drove dangerously in my haste to get to his place as soon as possible. On getting there, I rang the bell, but no one came to the door. I rang his mobile phone incessantly, yet no reply.

By now the panic button in my system had been pressed. Even as I write now, like any serious Christian, I am continually growing in the Lord, but at that time I was nowhere near where I am now in maturity and was thus reacting wildly to my senses.

To cut a long story short, I raised the alarm and someone with a spare key to Eze's residence was able to gain access to his place. Eze looked very confused and was very mute. I felt like crying but was thankful that we had come to his aid quickly.

I will not paint the picture of what I witnessed within the confines of his home as the memory is but a blur now—I asked the Holy Spirit to help me forget in order to move on. What I do remember is this, however. He appeared dazed, lost, and completely withdrawn, in fact almost completely immobile in his movements as he sat in one place like a statue. Now and again, he moved to another room, perhaps, but then resumed his stationary stance.

Trying to talk to him was like talking to a brick wall, for there was no response. Eze did not appear to have had slept much or at all. Yes, Eze seemed ill and what was most upsetting was that he did not appear to recognize me or anyone.

His cousin helped him dress, as by then he appeared helpless or perhaps uncooperative. The cousin took him off to the doctors, but not before I had begged the cousin not to allow the doctors to admit Eze to the hospital. Reluctantly, the doctor agreed that he could come home because his aunties would be staying over to look after him.

Several hours later in the day, I sat in my car. I had told a very understanding boss that I had an extreme emergency and would not be at work that day. By now, I urgently needed some fresh air. I had to get away from the depressing atmosphere that hung in Eze's place. I called my mother who lives in another country.

Thank God for godly counsel, especially if you have godly parents. My mother told me not to even think of leaving him or breaking the engagement. "It would be a serious mistake to do so," she warned. She counseled me to trust in God. I knew when I put the phone down that she would be praying. This brought me some relief and comfort.

However, all sorts of thoughts were whirling around my head by then. My mother was not the one who would have to live with Eze, I was reasoning. This was my life after all. I could take my chances—give him up in the hope that God would send someone else.

Just as I was contemplating those thoughts, my phone rang. It was a friend who at that time felt pressed in her spirit to give me the words that whatever I was thinking of doing, I should not do. Thank God for confirmation of the Holy Spirit.

Three or four weeks later, Eze "recovered." He had no recollection of what had happened on that fateful day nor the night before. He was now fully conscious of his environment and could recognize everyone. His aunts had returned to their individual homes, and Eze was now living by himself without any cause for anxiety or concern. I accompanied him to the doctor for a review and to be signed back into work. Eze was still not back to his "usual" self even at this point. He seemed very slow and his verbal communication sounded sluggish and deliberate, although as I later found out, the medication played a contributory factor in slowing him down.

I sat in the office observing the doctor questioning Eze. The doctor was very pleased that Eze had made progress and that he was back on his medication. In the meantime, I felt whipped. Medication was to me like a swear word.

"Under no uncertain terms must you ever stop taking this drug again!" the doctor said very sternly.

Something moved in my spirit. Goodness knows if this is what some people might call holy anger. But all I know was that I was not impressed!

The doctor was doing his job, but he certainly did not have the last word! God's Word was the last word in this. We would have to see to that, I determined.

Eze and I left the doctor's office shortly after with another prescription in hand for more medication. Right then, I determined that when I became his wife I would stand by this man no matter the cost. Wives, I knew from the marriage preparation classes we had been to, can help their husbands in whatever challenges they face.

Not many months after that episode, we got married. I was reluctant to postpone the date for the wedding. On what grounds anyway? Till he got well? No, I was certain that this was the man God had brought into my life, so I did not see the point of any delays. Yes, ours had been a whirlwind romance, as friends and acquaintances put it. We met and married within 11 months. But our individual pastors had met with us and given their blessings and approval. In fact, the wife of Eze's then-pastor took one look at me and told Eze she had been praying for him, smiled her approval, and went on to invite us for marriage preparatory classes. No long list of questions as I had imagined. I remember thinking at the time that Eze's pastor's wife must have thought I was the answer to her prayers by her comments. Later, that encounter was to give me comfort and assurance that I had made the right decision to stay. Those words became very pivotal in helping me weather the storms till the end. I would encourage you to always seek your pastor's or priest's approval before embarking on any major decision, especially marriage. It is certainly the best advice anyone can ever give you.

After we got married, I moved to Eze's church. A new branch had been started, and we joined that branch headed by a different pastor from the one Eze had been under. One day, this great man of God, our dearest pastor, gave me a sermon on marriage by a senior pastor of the ministry to which the church belonged. I went home, listened to the message, and that was that.

Then one day, several months later, I was listening to the message again when something struck within the chords of my spirit.

The senior pastor was expanding on the meaning of the word *helpmeet*, referring to Eve as the wife of Adam (see Gen. 2:18 KJV). The actual word helpmeet means "answer," the senior pastor was elaborating.

A light went on somewhere in my spirit. A candle had suddenly appeared in the dark. The senior pastor then said it plainly. Every wife is literally the answer for her husband.

This, therefore, meant I was the answer for Eze. That meant that whatever issues or challenges Eze faced, I was the answer. Obviously, Jesus is the answer to all life challenges. Don't misinterpret the point made. But what helpmeet means is that the wife helps the man in bringing the answer.

As wives you have the power to change things. You have the authority to stand in the gap for your husband and command the change. As one flesh you can take position and intercede on behalf of your husband and expect a change. Of course, the opposite is true too. Husbands and wives are one flesh; therefore husbands can do the same for their wives.

This meant and confirmed that Eze and I were truly in this together. This fight of faith could be done together.

How could one man chase a thousand, or two put ten thousand to flight, unless their Rock had sold them, unless the Lord had given them up? (Deuteronomy 32:30)

This is the power of agreement. And a man and his wife can do this each time there is an issue that needs to be dealt with. They can agree and cause changes—big changes. There is no comparison between one thousand and ten thousand! What a difference.

Two people are better off than one, for they can help each other succeed (Ecclesiastes 4:9 NLT).

I could help Eze succeed in this. The Bible backed me in this. The enemy now had to contend with me, and there was now more ammunition. That gave me the boldness I needed.

Perhaps you are thinking, *Well, good for you; I am not married.* Maybe you are a mother and your child is the one who has this evil disease to contend with. You can stand in the gap for your child. The power of agreement also applies. Friends can get together and agree. But whatever the case, prayerfully link up with someone you can trust. An agreement means that neither party has different agendas. You must have the same clear vision of your destination. You must both know what you are agreeing on.

Do two walk together unless they have agreed to do so? (Amos 3:3)

For example, one person can't be praying for you to reduce the medication while the other prays for you to come off the medication. Both prayers are good, but they are completely different things. If need be, write down what your prayer requests are based on and keep to it. Back your requests with Scriptures and agree. Last, for you men who declare yourselves to be confirmed bachelors, if I have not laid down a solid case on the benefits of marriage then goodness knows what else can convince you!

On a more serious note, there are benefits to marriage and one of the best is that you can both take your stand against the wiles of the devil and support each other in winning the fight of faith. The revelation of helpmeet located me on a different pedestal. I knew my rights as Eze's wife. And I sure was going to exercise my rights!

Another little step closer to victory!

Closing Thoughts

As a carer, never feel that asking for help is a sign of weakness. Faith is something that grows. As your faith grows, so does your ability. So don't be hard on yourself in this journey.

To the parents of the mentally ill, you are not a failure because of your child's condition. It is not your fault either. This is not the vengeance of God; you are not being punished for some old sin! You must not allow thoughts of condemnation that come from the devil to plague your thoughts. You cannot have thoughts of condemnation and walk by faith at the same time!

Carers may also feel lonely. Others can't understand their devotion and a life centered on the ones they are caring for. Never feel you are alone. Remember, God promised that He would never leave nor forsake us (see Heb. 13:5). As a child of God, there is one thing you can never be—alone. Remember His Presence. Abide in that Presence till those feelings of loneliness lift.

However, in all these points raised above, you must get or seek the support you need if you feel overburdened. The right support, not some new-age help that will only compound things. As we have established and keep repeating, the best place to start is in your church. The importance of being part of an assembly where God leads you cannot be overemphasized. God may lead you to other support groups, but first ensure you have the right foundation in your church.

Summary

1. Carers need support too. Ultimately, carers must remember they have God who cares for them. God is the Rock and Support in times of frustrations and despair.

2. A carer with a difference is one who has the Spirit of God (and hence the fruit of the Spirit including love and patience) and walks by faith and not sight (see 2 Cor. 5:7).

3. Carers may feel lonely. It is important, however, to remember that you can never be alone with God. Remember His Presence. Abide in that Presence till those feelings of loneliness lift.

4. Spouses can offer good support. There is power in the agreement of two. They can agree and cause changes, no matter what those mountains are.

5. A wife is a helpmeet. A helpmeet is the answer for her husband. Understanding that revelation gives a wife more confidence in her authority against satan.

Confession

I refuse discouragement. I refuse feelings of loneliness. The Lord is my strength. I am protected in His care. I have the ability to do all things. Nothing is impossible for me to achieve because the Lord is with me and in me. I have the wisdom to make the right decisions at all times. The Lord is my Helper. Therefore, doors of favor are open to me at all times. In Jesus' name, amen.

Chapter Six ——————————————————————

DEALING WITH FEAR AND ANXIETY

Negative Emotions

Worry, fear, anxiety, and panic attacks are all cousins. They all stem from the same family of negative emotions. The root of fear and anxiety is worry. When one thinks about it, a lot of people, even Christians, worry. People worry, for example, about when they will get to the hairdressers, if they'll catch the train on time, what school to send their kids to, and so on. This classification is the everyday worries of life. But Jesus challenged us not to even worry over these things!

> *Therefore I tell you, do not worry about your life, what you will eat or drink; or about your body, what you will wear. Is not life more than food, and the body more than clothes? Look at the birds of the air; they do not sow or reap or store away in barns, and yet your heavenly Father feeds them. Are you not much more valuable than they? Who of you by worrying can add a single hour to his life? And why do you worry about clothes? See how the flowers of the field grow. They do not labor or spin* (Matthew 6:25-28).

The next category of worriers is the category of chronic worriers. They worry incessantly. I am not sure if I ever fit in that category, but I was certainly somewhere in between the two classifications. For as long as I can remember, I was a classified a "worrier." In fact, even as a child I had perfected the art of worrying to a fine degree. I worried about everything and anything.

In the world we live in, it is very easy to be fearful or worried about something. There is always something negative on the news and media, be it war, earthquakes, the economy, or the latest scary scientific finding which always seems to contradict the findings before! For me, there was always something to focus my worry energy on. In fact, I remember a relative once telling me that if I were to lose my bus ticket it would perceived as a major disaster where I was concerned!

Of course, worriers don't enjoy worrying—well, I didn't. The sleepless nights, the lack of appetite, the negative thoughts doing Olympic sprints and so on—gosh, I longed to be free from the prison bars of worry. As we have established, worry never comes alone; it has cousins namely anxiety, doubt, and fear, to name a few. A very dangerous cocktail.

Negative emotions steal our inner peace and joy. These emotions are distressing. We don't function properly or think clearly when we are worried. In fact, First John says fear involves torment (1 John 4:18 NKJV). Other versions use the word "punishment." Strong's concordance even suggests an infliction—a penal infliction.

Yes, negative emotions punish our bodies and minds. Harmful chemical are released in our bodies that can impinge on our organs and cells in our entire body. This is why often when negative emotions are removed from our lives, many get physical healing miraculously, sometimes almost instantly.

What starts off as a negative thought eventually seeks to take control of our lives. These thoughts affect our behavior, our character, and eventually our destiny. Remember, the Bible says that as a person thinks, so are they (see Prov. 23:7). Negative emotions must be nipped in the bud. If not, why did Jesus come if we choose to be fearful, for example? Jesus, on leaving the earth, said He was leaving His peace (see John 14:27). The yoke of heaviness has been dealt with by Jesus. There is healing available to free you right now!

Face to Face With Fear

I tried so desperately hard to replace the cycles of worry with positive thinking, but that did not have much result or long-lasting effect. When I became a Christian in particular, I longed for the carefree life. Yes, I said carefree! Did not Jesus say after all that we must cast all our cares on Him? (See 1 Peter 5:7.) But that word had not become real to me—yet! I felt comfortable being the one in control of my cares. In fact, I formed a strategy that the best way to deal with worry was to always look at the glass as half empty instead of half full. That way there was always a backup plan in place in the event that the worst did in fact happen. I consoled myself that it meant I was ahead of the game and thus prepared for any eventualities. What a life! A hard life, when I think of it now.

Then I met Eze. God, the perfect Matchmaker, had positioned me to locate the man of my dreams. But like the children of Israel, when God gives you your Canaan, the land of promises, there are often giants in the land. When God gave me my husband, I knew our future would be flowing with milk and honey as Canaan was, as God had promised the Israelites. But I had not quite bargained for giants, real gigantic giants! I took one look into the supposed mirror of my future, which worry had started painting in the framework of mind, and found myself siding with the children of Israel. Yes, the Israelites had sided with the ten spies who brought back a negative report. So although by the time I met Eze I had been born again for a number of years, I certainly had not completely eliminated worry out of my life.

Because of my "track record" of worry, in the early days of our courtship I sought not to get too many details of Eze's medical history. For example, I never asked him what the diagnosis was or how many times he had been admitted to a mental hospital.

I am not quite sure if I was trying to sweep the whole thing under the proverbial carpet and in so doing hope that an "episode" would not occur. Or perhaps I knew my faith level was not strong enough to suppress the panic button that would be depressed if I knew the full facts. I suppose I did not want to kid myself. But you can't stop a bird from flying over your head. Trials are sure to come our way. In fact, Jesus told His disciples, "…In this world you will have trouble. But take heart! I have overcome the world" (John 16:33). I closed my eyes to the possibility of anything happening, while fear was heading my way in the meantime.

As I mentioned earlier, a few months before our wedding I came eyeball to eyeball with the evilness of the dark world of mental illness. I saw with my naked eyes everything I could possibly see. I sucked it all in, detail for detail. Naturally, I have an eye for detail, and you can be sure I did not miss any microscopic detail of what was happening to Eze. I had a clear-cut, three-dimensional picture that no doctor's report could vividly paint for me even if they tried. All on my own, all I had to do was close my eyes and the dark movie would start rolling. The devil had played poker and I was allowing myself to be sucked in hook, line, and sinker. The devil was now driving the car, with me as the passenger in the back seat. That meant he could take me anywhere he wanted as he pleased!

Did I take heart as Jesus said in the verse in John? On the contrary. I cannot pretend that I was not scared by what I saw. In fact I would not even attempt to mask it. I was petrified. Not of Eze, of course, because the illness did not manifest in any form of aggression or violence on his part. But I certainly did not like what I saw in him. In the days after the episode, I allowed my mind to dwell on the events of that day. Each time I closed my eyes, I replayed the movie picture of my Eze. With each playback, I was driving the images deeper within my soul and also my spirit. The spirit of fear was taking familiar abode!

To add insult to the already acute injury, I also allowed my mind to dwell on the statistics of mental illness. Statistics did not paint a good picture where recovery from mental illness was concerned. My brain was quick also to unearth a childhood discussion whereby I had been told that mental illness was one the most difficult diseases to treat. Nothing sounded or looked good. The odds, as they say, looked bad. And here I was face to face with the living realities of mental illness. What were my options?

As a self-confessed realist—for want of a better word than pessimist—I was going to learn something called optimism! In fact, I was going to learn F-A-I-T-H if I was to keep my sanity myself. Faith was the only real answer. No amount of positive thinking could condition my mind. Positive thinking would have to be a product of faith rather than the other way around. Was this God's sense of humor, I wondered? I for one was certainly not laughing!

> For God hath not given us the spirit of fear; but of power, and of love, and of a sound mind (2 Timothy 1:7 KJV).

Fear is much more than an emotion. Fear, as the verse above says, is a spirit, and one which God has not given His children. It has torment (see 1 John 4:18 NKJV). Fear keeps you in bondage. Fear makes you its slave. Fear gives room for the devil to plunder you further. Fear aims to keep you defeated. Fear holds you back, because God cannot perform in an atmosphere of fear. It is evil. Very evil. Need I go on?

Where Does Fear Come From?

So where does the spirit of fear come from?

Fear is real. It is not something you can wish away. Most times, it comes from what we allow our minds to focus on. Little negative thoughts and doubts soon grow into big negative thoughts, thus providing the right soil and environment for fear to take root.

Doubt is the ally of fear. Doubt provides the invitation for fear to come in. We must therefore be mindful of what we watch, read, listen to, or dwell on. This cannot be overemphasized. Many people have been bound with fear and not known where the root came from. Why then is it that after watching a horror movie, you find that you jump at every sound? Even the music we listen to can affect us, because music conveys a message, a very powerful message at that—we all know how music can affect our moods. Remember, music is spiritual whether good or bad.

For me, I had allowed myself to dwell on the negative pictures and facts of the disease. I looked at the statistics, the records, and the images. I spent more time on this than meditating on the Word, thus allowing the giants to look fearsome. And the fact is the more you are afraid, the more the devil manifests his tricks. Disregarding facts is not necessarily denial. Nor is it about being naïve or foolish either. Faith is not about denying the report of the doctor and experts as being wrong. Faith does not say "I do not have a headache" when one is feeling one. That would make faith a lie.

Faith speaks a different language than that. Faith declares instead "By the stripes of Jesus I am healed!" Instead of focusing on what the doctor and experts say, faith focuses on a higher law. The higher law of God's Word. And the Word is the truth (see John 17:17). The president of the ministry we belong to explains this illustration as follows. There is a law of gravity, but there is a higher law which is the law of lift. A higher law always dominates the lower! God's Word is therefore the last word.

You Have Power

"For God hath not given us the spirit of fear; but of *power*..." (2 Tim. 1:7 KJV). God is good. Many times in His Word He says, "Fear not."

Put yourself in the place of King Jehoshaphat in Second Chronicles 20 who was faced with a vast army from three nations who came to pick a fight against him. In verse 3, we are told that Jehoshaphat's first reaction was fear. Does that sound familiar? But I like what Jehoshaphat did when fear took hold of him—he inquired of the Lord.

No, Jehoshaphat did not gather the elders of Israel and have a pity or worry party. When the spirit of fear came knocking, Jehoshaphat remembered where power comes from! At that terrifying moment, Jehoshaphat reminded God and indeed himself that his God had power and might (2 Chron. 20:6). As an Old Covenant child of God, inherent power to cause the change from within him was not available, but he leaned on God. In your moments of weakness, when you are not conscious of the power that you have available to you as delivered to you by the finished works of Christ, do you still call on God? Or do you call a friend and bellyache the problem?

God would not tell us to do something if He has not given us the means to do so. What God has given us is power today. It is right here, right now in *you*. A study of the word "power" in Second Timothy 1:7 shows that it actually comes from the Greek word *dunamis*, which means ability to cause changes! That ability is in fact dynamic and not static.

So back to Jehoshaphat. When he called on God, guess what happened? God spoke through a prophet. And the first words God said were, "Do not be afraid." Praise God. Jehoshaphat had put the plug into the socket. Power, just like an electric plug, was now available to change his frightening situation.

Today, that same power is available within us. The big God of the universe has chosen His abode to be right inside your heart. There He lives in all His entirety. His power within us has the ability to change situations. That means we can face any challenge and win. The Word teaches us how to use that ability within us:

- Use the matchless name of Jesus

- Pray in and with the Spirit

- Put on the whole armor of God

- Walk in love

- Make the right confessions (We will examine this later.)

- Be joyful (see James 1:2)

You Have Love

"...and of *love*..." (2 Tim. 1:7 KJV). He has also given us love. Love comes from the Greek word *agape*. "There is no fear in love. But perfect love drives out fear, because fear has to do with punishment. The one who fears is not made perfect in love" (1 John 4:18). The devil loves strife. Strife and love don't walk together. Where there is strife, there is discord. Faith cannot function in such an environment. God moves in an atmosphere of love.

You Have a Sound Mind

"...and of a *sound mind*" (2 Tim. 1:7 KJV). Do you know you have the mind of Christ? (See Philippians 2:5 NKJV.) That mind is a sound mind! Now, of course, this was what I wanted for Eze and for myself. And this verse clearly spelt out that if I wanted a sound mind, fear would need to make an exit. If I chose to listen to negative information continually or even meditate on it for a minute, fear was sure to get hold of me. It was a question of making up my mind to sift into my mind only the right kind of information.

Like Moses told the children of Israel, I would have to keep the word in front of my eyes and on the doorpost in my heart in the midst of trouble. I would have to choose to dwell on the right thoughts if I was to walk in victory over fear (see Phil. 4:8). Fear would need to be out of my system if I was to be the helpmeet for my husband. If I was to be a pillar of support. As fear was a spirit, it was costly to allow it to linger in me and pass it on in my home, in Eze, and eventually in my marriage. Fear had to be arrested!

How You Read

I remember being offered a book on how to live with someone who had mental illness. I'll be blunt here. I never even saw what the cover of the book looked like. I politely declined the offer. What could any book tell me? Again, I am not denying the authenticity of whatever may have been written in such a book, but caution must be exercised even with what some "experts" say. Some suggestions, for example, may not be entirely biblical for a start; others could reinforce fear. Experts don't contain all the answers and experts make mistakes. Experts also contradict themselves with new findings or research. Choose such books wisely or extract whatever information you can from them. Remember, we have the Expert of all experts.

I knew that that book couldn't help *me*. Personally, I reasoned, to read such a book was accepting defeat. For me it was accepting that this was the status quo. It was accepting that we would have to manage the sickness instead of *taking authority* over it! I was not prepared to live with anyone who "had" mental illness any longer than I had to. The title of the book in itself was a wrong confession for me. So my question was: Why read the book? Can people take authority over a thief if they are prepared to live with or accommodate the thief?

No! I had a healthy expectation that our current predicament would end one day. I am in no way crucifying anyone who thinks such a book would prove useful. According to your faith be it. The Bible, I decided, was the Book that could tell me the answers I particularly wanted. The Bible is the light. "Your word is a lamp to my feet and a light for my path" (Ps. 119:105).

It is always prudent to be mindful of where and what type of information you read and more importantly *how* you read that information. Remember, scientific findings are always on the move and subject to change. Don't get me wrong—thank God for science, but be mindful how much you hinge on every word that science declares. Only a few decades ago, for example, science told us Pluto was a planet. Not so today; we are now told Pluto is a dwarf planet. One minute we are told margarine is good for us, the next it's butter, and so on and so forth.

Let God's Word be the main lamp. Anything you read must measure up to what God says in His Word. So if the books all say a particular disease you have been diagnosed with has a poor prognosis, thank God for the findings of science but use the greater light of God's Word to shine on that situation instead. I promise you, it will go a long way in building your faith!

Flex Those Faith Muscles

As I flexed my faith muscles, faith grew and fear started diminishing. The prison doors gave way and let the prisoner—me—out! Of course, when Eze and I got married I had to learn to deal with new fears that surfaced, such as having to check on Eze incessantly. No doubt that was not the solution in the long run, neither did he wish for me to have the burden of doing so. Also, as the head of the home he took his responsibility seriously and did not want the over-caring aspect of my love. I also ran the risk of damaging my own health.

You see, faith was the new giant growing in me. Faith was now taking root. And faith requires you to take your stand.

Like most people, Eze worried over some of the challenges in life that came his way. But like mine, his faith was also growing. I had cut off the supply of my fears feeding his, which helped him a great deal. His anxieties of when he would ever stop taking the medication became less pronounced. I reassured him that no matter what, I would remain his wife. In these modern times where marriage and divorce seem to be competing against each other, spouses need this kind of reassurance especially. For Eze, conquering worry was a major victory. Fear and worry are devil magnets. And where the devil is, his works are in operation. Fear and mental illness are buddies. Mental illness symptoms are exacerbated by fear. But Eze was making strides. Now when fear knocked, faith was at the door answering. Not only that, others began to see changes. Faith is visible.

Faith Is Visible

When Jesus heard this, He was amazed. Turning to those who were following Him, He said, "I tell you the truth, I haven't seen faith like this in all Israel!" (Matthew 8:10 NLT)

Jesus saw the faith of the centurion. Friends and family began to see our faith. They could see more evidence of joyful expectancy that things would work out in the end. And they could see faith working in our lives. Faith was producing results. Eze's mother felt more confident that Eze was making progress.

Would I say I have completely eradicated worry in my life now? Maybe not completely. If I am brutally honest, I probably have tiny crumbs to clear up. After being bound by fear for most of my life, getting rid of fear is not an overnight process. As we have established, there is an amount of deliberate self-training involved. However, one thing is for certain—I do not allow the birds to build a nest on my head. I know the antidote for fear and use it before fear even has a chance to get comfortable with me. I am still flexing my faith muscles. Isn't it this life of faith that we are called to live as Christians? Faith is our diet with the Word as our food. "And Jesus answered him, saying, It is written, That man shall not live by bread alone, but by every word of God" (Luke 4:4 KJV).

Yes, watch this space. Ask me soon and I'll tell you that even the crumbs of worry have vanished.

Closing Thoughts

Fear, worry, and anxiety are all negative emotions that have ill effects in us. The only way to effectively and permanently deal with attacks of negative emotions is to seek help from the Holy Spirit. Faith goes a long way in dealing with fear; but to cast out or expel fear, the Word of God has a slightly different agenda. Yes, that may shock our conventional thinking. No, God has said in His Word that it is *perfect love* that casts or drives out fear (see 1 John 4:18). I can deal with something without having driven it out, right? I can tell off a thief for being in my house, but that does not mean I have driven him or her out of my house, right? Yes, faith is what we need as the first step to deal with any contrary situation boldly and with confidence. I must have boldness to drive out that thief.

Love perfected in God means we come to the full awareness that God loves us so much we can trust Him completely. That is why God sent His Son, because of this love. His Son paralyzed satan and made him powerless. If we occupy our mind with those thoughts, we can yield to God and allow Him to guide and protect us. We can listen out for Him to warn us when there are any impending dangers, because He most certainly will. That way all tricks of the devil are thwarted. Satan just ends up chasing his tail instead of Christians and unbelievers who do not know these things. Often, we are too busy working out our own lives to pick up what the Holy Spirit is trying to transmit to us. No, we must instead trust God's love and then we won't have fear. If you are in fear, then you are not in that trust yet.

Fear is an avenue for the devil to have his free reign. When you are in fear, you are telling the devil in effect that you are vulnerable. You might as well go ahead and tell the devil to hit you! That is exactly what happened to Job. He fretted too much and half expected the evil that came to him to come. See for yourself what he says here:

> *What I feared has come upon me; what I dreaded has happened to me* (Job 3:25).

Don't be like Job. Yes, he was a righteous man, but he lived a life of fear. So much that he was always doing sacrifices in case any of his children sinned. What a life! But let's not be quick to point fingers at Job. Many of us do. We plan for every eventuality—"what ifs" that never even happen. Why not trust God's love instead?

When fear tries to attack your mind, rebuke it. Give fear no place in your life. Speak faith into that situation. Put some words into that situation. No, faith is not about positive thinking. It is Word thinking! Just have stubborn faith.

Summary

1. Fear, worry, and anxiety are all negative emotions that are harmful to our minds and bodies.

2. We have inherent power (*dunamis*) inside us to cause changes to any situation.

3. We have love. When we trust in God's perfect love, we know that God is taking care of us.

4. We have a sound mind.

5. Use the greater light of God's Word to guide you in how you read and process information.

Confession

I refuse to fear. I refuse to dread. I have a sound mind—that mind is the mind of Christ. God said I should not be anxious about anything, so I am doing as He says from today. I choose instead to trust Him. There is an anointing in my life that causes me to think right. Those thoughts chart my life on the right path. Those thoughts inspire me. I have power working in me. I rest in God's love. I cast out fear in my life. The Word of God infuses boldness in me. The Word energizes me, propels me, moves me forward and upward only. I cannot be defeated in anything. God says I am a success. My name is success. I walk in God's love today and every day. My future is bright. Thank You, Jesus. Amen.

Chapter Seven ─────────────────────────────

Saying the Right Thing

Sticks and Stones

Sticks and stones will break my bones but words won't hurt me. Really?

Remember how we used to chant, "Sticks and stones can break my bones but words won't hurt me" in the playground as kids? How untrue for the Christian! In fact, I firmly believe the opposite is true. Sticks and stones should not break our bones as Christians, because we have the life of God in us that makes us stand strong in the face of adversity.

God does not make weaklings. See how David challenged a giant—Goliath, the Philistine (see 1 Sam. 17). See how King Jehoshaphat fought three strong nations that came against his nation (see 2 Chron. 20). But if we were to examine the words of David and also King Jehoshaphat in our examples above, you will see that when faced with terrifying situations they chose their words carefully. They did not say things like, "I just knew this would happen"—the words of doom some of us prophesy into our lives. Neither did they start charting a dangerous course for the events by wrong words such as, "This is really bad. The odds don't look good!"

No! How could they? David was so courageous that he made his eldest brother Eliab burn with anger. David's boldness made the entire army of Israel look like toy soldiers. His first words to the giant Goliath showed what this man was made of:

> *David said to the Philistine, "You come against me with sword and spear and javelin, but I come against you in the name of the Lord Almighty, the God of the armies of Israel, whom you have*

defied. This day the Lord will hand you over to me, and I'll strike you down and cut off your head..." (1 Samuel 17:45-46).

Goodness, David threatened to cut off the head of the Philistine, yet he had no spear. All the young David had in his hands were five stones. And as we read later in the story, what he proclaimed indeed came to pass.

David ran and stood over him. He took hold of the Philistine's sword and drew it from the scabbard. After he killed him, he cut off his head with the sword... (1 Samuel 17:51).

No one would have blamed David for feeling an ounce of fear, but even if he did (which I am sure he didn't, by the way), he surely had a great way of hiding it. He deliberately spoke the right words. That's the mentality of a winner. And you can do the same.

Eze's First Appointment

"Do you smoke cannabis?"

"No."

"Do you hear voices?"

"No."

"Have you ever felt like killing yourself?"

"Certainly not!"

This is crazy, Eze thought to himself as the psychiatrist fired her questions like bullets out of a gun. This was Eze's first appointment at the outpatient clinic soon after his discharge from his first admittance at the mental hospital. As he recounted the dialogue to me, I could only imagine how distressing things might have seemed for him at the time.

He was at that time fully dosed on all manner of prescription drugs, causing him to feel drowsy most of the time. Interestingly, in some ways he felt at peace, but it was a false peace derived from the medicines. Yet he couldn't associate the questions being asked with the person they were asking—namely himself. He was flabbergasted.

Even so, Eze had a strong determination. Back then he used his self-will to overcome the world of psychiatry. Although it takes more than self-determination and self-will to overcome mental illness, it was at least a good initial start. In Eze's heart, he repeatedly thought and longed to be free, to escape this dark world. He tried within the limited capacity we have as humans not to entertain thoughts that mental illness was his lot in life.

But not everyone is like Eze. Not everyone has that kind of determination.

What do you say when a psychiatrist is firing such questions at you? Questions you want to block out of your brain? How do you say the right things when the wrong things are being said all around you? It is bad enough when people criticize us; we all know how that feels. It can create insecurities in some or a sense of inferiority. And inferiority can cause us to say the wrong things. How do you maintain your composure when others bring you bad tidings?

The ten spies brought back an evil report from Canaan to the children of Israel. They outnumbered the two who came back with a good report that God was all they needed. But the children of Israel did not need much ado to start screaming and shouting words of defeat. I can imagine the pandemonium on that day. (See Numbers 13 and 14.)

How different is that scene from the world today? How do Christians say the right thing when everyone is saying the wrong thing or using the wrong words? When everybody else has an evil report?

How do you refuse to say the wrong thing and refuse to echo what God did not say?

> *The tongue has the power of life and death, and those who love it will eat its fruit* (Proverbs 18:21).

I remember once being reprimanded by the Holy Spirit. I knew the words in my spirit came directly from God, telling me to season my words with grace. I knew God was not happy with my speech some of the time. I remembered someone once saying it is not what is said that is often offensive but how it is said. The warning from the Holy Spirit was certainly a rain check for me to sit up and tidy up my communication, especially in relation to my husband for whom I knew the warning had stemmed from.

> *Let your conversation be always full of grace, seasoned with salt, so that you may know how to answer everyone* (Colossians 4:6).

I imagined Paul in the verse in Colossians warning the Colossians to be careful what they talked about. Salt preserves. "Seasoned with salt" means our speech *must* bring healing. In Proverbs it says, "Pleasant words are a honeycomb, sweet to the soul and healing to the bones" (Prov. 16:24). There it is in black and white. Kind words have the power to heal. Frustration of any kind was therefore no excuse for me to speak unpleasantly or even sharply in anger to my husband. In fact, with discipline, as my faith muscles were flexed, frustration ceased to be in my dictionary. I learned to always minister to my husband with grace, regardless of the pressures I felt as his so-called "carer" whenever an episode occurred. This grace was the goodness, blessing, and favor of God.

"Seasoned with salt" also means ensuring our words have flavor. Good flavor. It is more than not swearing.

"I am not *too* bad," is one example of words lacking flavor. These are most certainly not words full of grace. But even Christians confess this all the time and then wonder why things are not *too* bad. In effect, what they are saying is that things are bad but could have been worse. Think about it!

We must be choosy about our words, because words are spirit. Words have the power to bring to pass things we speak concerning ourselves. It is a spiritual law. The president of the ministry that our church is part of always says this: "Your mouth is not for talking and eating only. Our mouth has been given to us to chart our course in life!"

Confession of God's Word

Thank God for such truths. Thank God for the teachings of this man of God who teaches to never talk sickness but talk health all the time. What we say in life is what we will get. The Greek word for "confession" is *homologia*, which means speaking the same thing in consent or agreement with God.

God certainly did not say Eze was ill, so how could I confess it irrespective of the doctor's report? I encouraged Eze to stop taking possession of the illness with the use of the word "my," as in "my sickness." Every good and perfect gift is from God (see James 1:17). God certainly does not use evil on His kids or the devil's tools to correct His children. That does not sound like a good God! You wouldn't use a gun, something that can kill, to correct your children, would you? Therefore this sickness was not Eze's to keep, I encouraged.

To speak the same thing in agreement with God would mean speaking about "my health" instead. Don't you agree? We need to know what God says concerning us in His Word.

As Eze and I studied the Word individually and together, we started learning to memorize Scriptures. Memorizing Scriptures helped us in saying the right thing. Taking footsteps of faith is directly correlated to the words we speak. Eze and I needed to confess that which we hoped for in order to get our victory. A bonus therefore of saying the right thing is that it helps our faith.

> *Let us hold fast the confession of our hope without wavering, for He who promised is faithful* (Hebrews 10:23 NASB).

God's promises are infallible. And those infallible promises are what faith demands. After all, did He not promise such things as:

> *He Himself bore our sins in His body on the tree, so that we might die to sins and live for righteousness; by His wounds you have been healed* (1 Peter 2:24).

> *He heals the brokenhearted and binds up their wounds* (Psalm 147:3 NKJV).

Our pastor in his many sermons taught us how to talk to our bodies, teaching them to respond to the words we speak. The president of our ministry revealed how Jesus spoke to a fig tree, to storms, and so on. He expatiated that if Jesus told us in Mark 11:23 to talk to the mountain, that means we could speak to anything, be it animate or inanimate. Another man of God also said once instead of talking about any illness attacking our body we could instead choose to talk to it!

The Word of God certainly has power. On one particular occasion when Eze was feeling battered by the symptoms of yet another attack, Eze searched the Scriptures and this became his favorite.

> *For the word of God is living and active. Sharper than any double-edged sword, it penetrates even to dividing soul and spirit, joints and marrow; it judges the thoughts and attitudes of the heart* (Hebrews 4:12).

There we have it. The Word can reach your body in parts that medicine cannot reach easily, such as the marrow. It can reach parts medicine cannot reach such as your spirit—the human spirit. The spirit is the real you—who we really are—for we are spirit beings living in a body. The Word can reach your soul, which is your mind, emotions, intellect, and will. In its entirety the Word can heal your spirit, soul, and body. What medicine has the ability to do so? The King James Version of the verse in Hebrews actually says the Word of God is quick! Eze chewed on this Scripture, and on that particular occasion meditating and confessing that Scripture certainly sped up his recovery time!

By this time Eze and I knew how to recognize the very early symptoms, even in their faintest form, and consequently deal with them. Early symptoms could include simple things like the fact he was not sleeping well, for sleep was never a problem for him. Other first signs included feeling slightly agitated or restless and symptoms of sharp pain. There were also some instances of paranoia or an uncommon boldness in his speech which could be perceived as cheeky or slightly aggressive, words which are completely against Eze's character. As these symptoms appeared, we shone the light on God's Word and confessed these words with our mouths.

Confessing God's Word became easier as time progressed. Eze and I were confessing words such as the following and even much more:

> *"I have the life of God in me—in my bones, my head, my blood, in every fiber and cell of my body. I am infused with the Word of God from the crown of my head to the soles of my feet. My body is the temple of the Holy Spirit, therefore no sickness can fasten itself to my body. Greater is He who is in me than he that is in the world. I have the mind of Christ. The wisdom of God is working in me. My life is for the Glory of God."*

I must add that confessing did not mean just saying those words quietly within our hearts. No, we had to say them out loud. Why?

As I mentioned before, we are often affected by the words we hear. When we confess the words out loud rather than quietly within our hearts, we make our ears hear the words we speak. And faith then comes (see Rom. 10:17). Also, saying words out loud drowns out our thoughts. It is almost impossible to think and say different things at the same time! If you don't believe that, try it now yourself. You'll discover you'd soon start saying whatever you were thinking or your speech would not be fluent, paused by the thoughts in your mind.

You see as a man thinks, so is he. And the chances are we are likely to speak out what's on our minds the most. What you say flows from what is in your heart (see Luke 6:45 NLT). We can only speak the words we think. Joyce Meyer says we must think about what we're thinking about! For me, that means classifying your thoughts. Are your thoughts lies from satan or truths of God's Word?

So even though Eze's health did not instantly change the nanosecond he confessed those words, the wheels were certainly in motion. He was becoming the words he spoke.

Speak It Out Loud

I also advocate speaking out loud to the devil. Jesus certainly was not quiet when He rebuked demons. Others heard Him! Eze and I learned to openly rebuke the devil, be it in public or private. Anyway, people may have already formed their opinions on Eze's mental health, so what difference would it make if some stranger now thought we were crazy for speaking out loud and telling the devil where to get off?

If Eze felt a symptom of an attack, he learned to address satan and his demons with words like, "Devil, I rebuke you in the name of Jesus!" Likewise, when worried thoughts or doubts wanted to cram my mind, depending on the degree of worry I would even scream out, "In the name of Jesus, I refuse to worry. Get behind me satan!"

Kenneth Hagin, in his book *What to do When Faith Seems Weak and Victory Lost*, speaks of his mother's episodes of psychiatric history. In this book, he says his mother's doctor advised her to resist and refuse the attacks. He told her she could do more for herself than any medication. I remember reading that and thinking how incredible and powerful. This means doctors know that medication does not have the answer. Anyway, Hagin went on to quote Ephesians 6:13, "...having done everything, to stand." When his mother felt an attack, she resisted the attack by talking to herself, saying, "No, I am not going to have an attack!" Fifty years later, she'd never had a further spell. Praise God! There is certainly power in the words of a believer.

Devils tremble and shake at the mention of the name of Jesus from the mouth of a believer. This is why it is important for a believer to know who he or she is and also know with all certainty what their rights are. If you don't know what your rights are, you can believe anything. In some countries, even if you are a stranger in the land you are told that ignorance of their law is no excuse. So if you commit a crime, you would be punishable according to the judicial system, with no allowance made that you were not aware of the law. Likewise, a Christian who does not know their rights has no excuse when the devil decides to whack you like a tennis ball. Know your rights!

Consistency Is the Key

Consistency in speaking right is also important. Many people become skeptics of the teachings on confession when they do not immediately see the changes they desire. What many forget to realize is that they have spent years and decades saying the wrong thing and expect a change in the circumstances overnight.

No, I do not believe that if you have been saying the wrong thing consistently for twenty years that consequently means that you are going to spend the next twenty years repairing the damage. Remember, the Word is *living and active* (see Heb. 4:12). If you keep applying force to a wall consistently, eventually that wall will come tumbling down. It's the same principle with our confessions. Eze and I confessed the Word twice daily, minimum! For starters, we always started and ended the day right by making our declarations of God's promises. We spoke the right things to each other. I constantly encouraged his faith by speaking the right words to him instead of confessing any negative pictures that attempted to come to my mind.

Perhaps you are thinking you have always been speaking negatively. Maybe you are even beginning to see the fruits of those negative words in your life. Don't lose heart. Take courage. The same way you got yourself wound up in the situation you are in through careless or even deliberate words is the same way you can unwind yourself out of that situation. It is never too late. Nothing is too late with God. He is a merciful and gracious God.

Clearly you can see that Eze was way ahead on the path to his divine healing and health through the steps he was taking. We were not "there" yet, but we had come a long way!

Closing Thoughts

Even our everyday English language is rife with words of unbelief, such as:

Wrong talk	What we are actually saying
I am dying to meet you.	See how we speak death.
I am afraid I can't help you.	See how we speak fear.
You little devil.	The devil is not one you want to be like!
I am sick and tired of this job.	See how we speak sickness and tiredness.
I am in need of this.	A Christian must never confess any need.
I have a headache.	Why are you possessing a headache? Can't you just feel a headache instead?

We have to reprogram our speech to speak words that bring life instead of death. Jesus never spoke like some of the examples we saw above, so why should we? He spoke differently, so much so His disciples did not understand Him when he said Lazarus was sleeping. Jesus on that occasion did not want to speak to them carnally. He spoke from the Spirit instead of the flesh, and that was the reason He always got results. If we want to live the life of Jesus and get these same results, we must follow His example and change our words. We must choose our words carefully if we want to live strong and healthy. You don't have to be sick to die either. So avoid sickness whether you are 25 or 90 years old!

Yes, you can stay young in the Word of God. Learn to say what you want to come to pass. You are not going to get your healing if you keep talking sickness, even carelessly. You get what you say! Stay with the Word till every symptom is gone.

Even when every symptoms leaves your body, you must still speak right. Keep speaking health and healing. Your mouth may have got you in the wrong situation, but you can change that. Don't just go back to talking wrong.

Here's a final thought that will nail the point of speaking right. Scientists, researchers, and the like have carried out numerous researches and findings into the correlation between speech and our body. Some of their findings are quite startling in that our words carry power beyond our imagination. Medical researchers today even claim that the part of the brain that controls our speech controls every nerve of our body. Definitely food for thought!

Finally, don't say or even think, "What will be!" It will only be if you don't say anything, so steer your life in the right direction with the correct words!

Here's a word for your meditation: *"If you don't like what you have, change what you are saying!"*

Summary

1. Words are powerful. We must be mindful of the words we speak.

2. The Greek word "confession" is *homologia*, which means speaking the same thing in consent or agreement with God.

3. Instead of talking *about* any illness attacking our body, we could instead choose to talk *to* it!

4. Consistency in speaking right is also important.

5. Remember the Word is *living and active* (see Heb. 4:12). If you keep applying force to a wall consistently, eventually that wall will come tumbling down. It's the same principle with our confessions.

6. Don't be a quiet Christian. Jesus was not quiet when He rebuked devils.

Prayer

Father, forgive me for those times when I have not spoken right. Holy Spirit, help me to use my tongue in the right way. Instead of speaking words of defeat and fear, I speak words of faith and words full of life. I deliberately choose to speak words of a king from this day forth. I change the course of my life with the Word of God. As I do, I uplift and bless others. I season my words with grace. In Jesus' name, amen.

Chapter Eight —————————————————————————————

CELEBRATING MILESTONES

Two and half years after Eze and I met he was still on medication, although much reduced to perhaps taking the drugs once or twice a week. Occasionally, he was still having one or two episodes or symptoms of attack every five to six months, though with each attack the recovery period was reduced. His healing was certainly underway, though he was not completely healed.

I am sure some may think if the battle had not been won entirely, then until it was there were no victories to celebrate. That couldn't be further from the truth!

A two-and-a-half year journey of recovery after at least fourteen years of torment was definitely something to shout about. God's presence in our lives was strongly manifesting. Eze not only felt different, he looked different.

Here are some the testimonies of the changes that took place steadily over that period:

- Soon after Eze and I started dating, the social worker who visited him monthly to check up on him acknowledged that Eze no longer required his services, citing that he dealt with cases far more serious than his. The social worker was then signed off.

- Eze started reducing his dosage gradually. Five milligrams was reduced to alternating every other day with five milligrams and two and a half milligrams. After a period of time, Eze came off the five milligrams completely and only went on it when he felt symptoms. He then started taking the two and a half milligrams daily. As his faith grew, usually after an attack, he reduced the dosage again to taking two and a half milligrams on alternate days only.

Eze's doctor was obviously not happy with this self-medication, but we were exercising our faith and we were being led by the Holy Spirit every step of the way. Our pastor was kept informed every step of the way too. It is important that you are clearly hearing from God and seeking the right spiritual guidance. Dr. Frederick Price wrote a book called *Faith, Foolishness or Presumption*. Make sure it is not the latter two you are exercising. It has to always be nothing else but faith. Don't misunderstand the message of faith.

- With a completely new wardrobe, Eze's posture had changed remarkably to reflect the changes in his life. His demeanor altered. I noticed when I met him that his head was mostly slanted to one side and that he twiddled his thumbs a lot, making him appear sad. Because we are social beings, a large percentage of our communication is usually visual and non-verbal contact. But with the Word transforming Eze, I noticed that attitudes of people toward Eze started altering. His boss complimented Eze on his transformation, and soon his colleagues started interacting with him much more too.

- His voice changed, sounding more perky, alert, and bright. His parents and siblings were noticing that he sounded happier on the phone.

- Mind blankness was itself now drawing a blank. This was particularly meaningful for Eze. There were times beforehand when he told me he felt like his head was being clamped.

I also remember going on a church seminar once with him before we married. We were asked to do an exercise by answering a few questions. I was busy steaming ahead writing down my answers. I had finished writing on the first page and was about to go onto the second when I turned to see how he was doing. His paper was still blank and he was twirling his pen between his thumb and index finger. Everyone else was busy writing. I asked Eze what the matter was, to which he told me that as much as he was thinking very hard, his mind was drawing a blank. I knew this to be a demonic attack. That day I vowed that once we got married, satan would know it was now a new order; he would have me to contend with in taking his filthy hands off my husband's mind. I was extremely angry. This was definitely holy anger. How could a smart guy like Eze come to a point where he was not able to think at all?

- He started reading more, and as his reading capacity increased he read books to completion. In the early years after he had been diagnosed with mental illness, Eze had bought countless books which he either never read or started reading but never went past the first page. In fact, at his worst low, Eze found he just could not read at all. The devil is wicked, make no joke about that. But after being prayed for and ministered to by his first pastor, Eze received his healing for this. Praise God! He even passed a difficult exam, one in which the failure rate is quite high.

- His concentration increased. Being an excellent note-taker, I taught Eze the art of how to listen while taking good notes. In no time, he started taking notes in church, and that spilled over later to taking minutes at meetings at work.

- His short-term memory also increased. By now he was memorizing a lot of Scriptures, the definite cure for this!

- During the period he was on five milligrams, he started feeling less drowsy even with the medication. Eze stopped sleeping altogether in church and at work meetings. Eze trained his body to respond to the words he spoke over his body and not according to how he felt, which was sleepy most of the time.

- He lost the artificial weight which the medication had caused him to gain.

- Frequent minor ailments such as skin rashes, colds, fever, and so on became infrequent before eventually disappearing. There seemed to be always one ailment or another Eze had to deal with. At one time, he had a severe attack of gout.

- He developed a more positive outlook in life while at the same time talking less of the medals of his past.

- He took on new interests and became a vital worker in our church.

- Instead of continuing to pay into health insurance, he cancelled the payments and used the money to partner with healing programs in the ministry our church belonged to and in other ministries too.

- He also started paying his tithes and giving seeds. This was a landmark for Eze, as it meant that money no longer had a hold on him.

Before I met him, Eze kept his pockets tightly reined and believed within himself that he was being careful with his resources. However, I pointed out to him that money was instead "leaking" from his pockets. It always seemed that there was one thing or another that would cause him to spend money he had not planned for or budgeted. He had even made large investments into schemes that either folded or never amounted to anything. Years beforehand, he had even taken on extra weekend work to clear a large amount of debt.

But then the Word of God says when we bring our tithes He will rebuke the devourer for our sakes (see Mal. 3:10-11). Money is spiritual, whether you accept it or not. Initially, Eze refused to accept listening to me that if he paid his tithes he would see a difference in his money. Mathematically, it did not make sense. But we are not talking about mathematics here. These are the deep things of the spirit. And the spiritual governs the natural, believe it or not.

I had to challenge Eze to at least try it and see. Even God said, "Test Me in this…" (Mal. 3:10). Thank God Eze listened eventually.

And wasn't the devourer rebuked? Eze began to see things around him breaking down less, his household maintenance bill reduced drastically, he stopped making poor investment decisions, and he also stopped making other costly mistakes.

Don't be sceptical about tithes. And your offerings too. There is a law on giving. Have you ever thought why the rich get richer? Rich people who give always get more, whether they are Christians or not. See how many charities they sponsor and see how lavishly some of them give. Deep down they have learned this principle. And God always honors a giver. So the rich keep getting richer while the poor man who says he has nothing to give stays poor. Much food for thought there, I think. Don't you?

Step by Step

Right, back to Eze's milestones. With all the evident things happening to Eze and around us, it was impossible not to be thankful even though we had not reached our final destination. How could we not give praises to His name for all the wondrous things He was doing? How could we not celebrate each milestone by sharing the testimonies with others?

If the woman with the issue of blood had not come forward and told *all* her story when Jesus asked who had touched Him, we would not have known of the woman's suffering and been blessed by her testimony today. No doubt, I am sure Jairus, the ruler of the synagogue whose daughter Jesus was going to heal, must have had his faith stirred up too. Hearing this woman must have given Jairus hope for his own desperate situation of his one and only daughter who was dying. (Read the whole account of these stories in Luke 8:40-56.)

The woman with the issue of blood had been to many doctors before who couldn't help her. But this woman *knew* she was healed when she touched Jesus' garment. The knowledge within her that she was healed was not derived after she had been to a check up to the very same doctors who had diagnosed her and tried to treat her. No. And because of her testimony she went from being healed to being made whole. But there will be more time to talk about the importance of testimonies later.

The only way to keep moving was by celebrating our milestones. Oh, yes the devil did not come and congratulate us each time we did. That would be a first if he did. On the contrary. In fact, he stepped up his ammunition. Sometimes after sharing a testimony, not many days would pass before Eze would start having symptoms or have a full-blown attack.

But the devil is a fool. Believe me, he is. What the devil does not realize is that each time he comes with such pranks he is only aiding us in getting to our destination quicker, provided we don't quit on God. No, don't be scared of satan. You are not scared of a fool, so don't be scared of satan. You see, like a typical two-year-old throwing a tantrum, as the devil was increasing his attacks we were only being propelled forward. As I said before, the recovery times were getting shorter after every attack and that was a sure boost for our faith. This meant Eze and I were on a roll. Faith was growing. We were getting bolder. We were accelerating now. With the devil's ploy aiding us forward and even faster to our final destination.

What a fool he is!

Closing Thoughts

Everyday people around the world celebrate milestones. We celebrate birthdays, anniversaries, and so on. Why do we do this? People celebrate for different reasons but usually to express our joy over certain things. There is usually a sense of achievement that goes with celebrations.

Celebrating milestones will help you in your journey of faith. It helps because it diverts focus on the journey that is still ahead of us. Instead, we are encouraged when we see how far God has taken us. It is a right thing to do to show appreciation for the marvels of God in our lives.

Remember the devil will keep bombarding your thoughts with the wrong suggestions. He'll even try to make you feel that whatever you have attained is by coincidence or that that it happens to everyone else. But so what; you must challenge him. What is the big deal if millions have apparently been able to achieve "effortlessly" what you seemed to take an age to do? It is still important to God and therefore to you. Nothing, no matter how small, is ever trivial to God. Absolutely nothing. If God numbers each strand of your hair, how much more the works of God in your life.

The fact that you can wriggle a finger even though you cannot move your hand is a major cause for celebration nonetheless. It means healing has started! The fact that you have found a part-time job in the post office for now even though you desire a job at NASA is still something to shout about. Why? Because it means the Word is gaining ground in your life.

Why celebrate that little milestone that no one thinks is a big deal? Because the Word says that God, who has begun a good work in you, shall carry it unto completion (see Phil. 1:6). In fact, the apostle Paul said he was very confident of this very thing—that the work will be seen to the end. Check it, it is right there in the beginning of that verse. God does not do half-finished jobs.

In fact, it pays to be confident in our trust of God. The Bible further tells us not to cast away our confidence. In fact, there is a promise for those who don't. They will get their reward. I like how the New Living Translation puts it:

> *So do not throw away this confident trust in the Lord. Remember the great reward it brings you!* (Hebrews 10:35 NLT)

There is a reward at the end of this journey. Ignore the potholes along the way. Keep plodding and have a thankful heart. The devil can't stand anyone who is thankful. He is allergic to godly praise. Remember how the walls of Jericho came down with praise (see Josh. 6). He gets whipped with praises to God. That is why praise and thanksgiving should always be on the lips of a believer. And this is why satan will discourage you from celebrating the good things God has done in your life.

The devil knows that a thankful heart is one that gets more done than an ungrateful one. There is a story of Jesus and ten lepers. Jesus instructed them to go show themselves to the priest even though they were in their leprous state. Now in those days, a leper was certified healed by the priest, so it took a great amount of trust and faith in Jesus for them to yield to His instruction. Yet the sad thing about that story is that only one came back and said thank you to Jesus. That is like many Christians who take off and stop going to church as soon as they get what they want, even though God has got greater and bigger plans in store for them. Well, the one leper who came back with thanks was the one who went from healing to being made whole. Yes, the others were made clean, but they would still have the scars of leprosy, the deformed digits and so on to look at as a constant reminder of their past. But this one man, because he celebrated his milestone, had everything restored.

It certainly pays to celebrate milestones!

Summary

1. The devil is not going to celebrate your progress. In fact oftentimes, he steps up his ammunition after a testimony is shared. However, this just moves us closer to our destination.

2. If the devil tries to discourage you, just get bolder.

Prayer

Thank You, Father, for all You have done in my life. Thank You for what You are doing now and for the things to come. I will always maintain a thankful and grateful heart, because You are so good. Thank You for the everyday testimonies in my life. As I maintain a grateful heart, I am confident of this very thing—that You who have begun a good work in me will see it to completion. In Jesus' name, amen.

Chapter Nine —————————————————————————————

STICKING WITH THE WORD

Don't Give Up

Thomas Edison's story is one of a man who refused to give up. His story will motivate you.

Edison was an inventor. He invented the first incandescent light bulb. The stories differ on the number of attempts it took, but one thing is consistent—he made a great deal of attempts. A reporter once asked him after many years of apparently fruitless efforts in inventing the light bulb, "How does it feel to fail a thousand times?"

Edison replied, "I have not failed once. I am just a thousand steps closer to the solution." Some versions say that Edison replied that he had *successfully* found a thousand ways to not make a light bulb. What an answer. Edison did not consider himself a failure. Yet a look at Edison's childhood—his teachers did not think much of him. Yet today, the world can thank the man who went a long way in lighting up our homes.

How many unsuccessful attempts have you made? Are you even up to 100 yet? Feeling worn down already? Then think of Edison. Think of characters in the Bible like David who refused to give up. He was anointed king but crowned king several years later. In the meantime, he endured a lot of persecution and went through countless trials while often fleeing for his life. It must have seemed that he would never become king. But David became king, ruling Israel for 40 years.

Refuse to give up. Refuse to give in.

Don't Change Your Confession

"If you stick with the Word, you'll come back with a testimony."

These were the words of my pastor's wife to me about six months after Eze had come off the medication and nearly three years after we first met. These were the same words Eze and I had been accustomed to hearing from the president of our ministry through his video messages. But now those words were more real. More alive, more applicable to me. Applying that word was a case of now or never.

Eze had suffered a setback. A stressful situation at work had precipitated into an endless cycle of worry and fear.

As we have established earlier, fear is the fertile ground for the enemy to work in. Apart from that, I had discovered that the slightest sign of Eze getting worried over anything was a slippery slope for his health. If not arrested immediately, it could spell an attack. In the past, I had learned to detect the early signs of an attack. The slowed speech, being withdrawn, and lack of sleep. But this time I had not had an inkling that something was happening till he spoke up a few weeks prior and told me that he was very worried about changes in his work environment. As he spoke then, I noticed that indeed his facial expressions looked very strained, though that did not raise much concern for me.

Certainly, when he alerted me to his issues I encouraged Eze with the Word, reminding him of the milestones he had achieved so far. He had come a long way—too far, in fact. He was familiar with the tricks of the devil by now. He had enough of God's Word in him to be able to divert any negative situation or even the possibility of any symptoms. I was confident that we had built a strong foundation on the promises of God for his health. If the familiar storms were to come again, I was certain the foundation should remain unshaken.

But with each passing day, I noticed Eze getting more withdrawn. He started having sleepless nights too. He took a long time in answering questions. The symptoms were definitely back.

But we were determined to exercise our faith even further this time. Eze decided he would avoid taking the medication, which usually had to be stepped up in the event of an attack to *at least* five milligrams. We maintained our confessions in spite of what we could see.

Then, bang! I called him at lunch time at work only to find he was on his way home. His boss had sent him home. I tried ascertaining what had happened only for Eze to abruptly end and switch his phone off. This was so untypically his behavior. My heart was pounding. My heart refused to believe what my head was telling me was happening. Hey, I was a faith giant, wasn't I? I needed to keep calm. Angels were protecting him right now. They would bring him home safely. He hadn't sounded confused…or had he?

I refused to analyze the few words we had spoken just minutes before. I refused to look for signs of anything amiss. This was the Word at work now. I would have to choose faith over worry. Come on, Eze and I had given several testimonies of God's goodness with regard to Eze's healing so far, hadn't we? The testimony of God's Word stood, *didn't it?*

I dashed home to silence the several questions that were now competing for space in my brain. I made a quick phone call to my pastor's wife to alert her that Eze was not feeling well again. I sighed disappointedly.

Thankfully, we only lived a few miles away from my place of work. All the while as I was doing my James Bond maneuvers on the road, I kept praying and confessing the Word all the way. I put the keys through the front door and sucked in my breath.

I knew he was home. I could see his shoes and bag by the front door. I called out to him. His reply sounded like he was almost annoyed. My Eze never sounded annoyed unless he felt ill. What more proof did I need now? My heart felt like it was about to escape from its rib cage.

Eze sat in the kitchen sipping something. I asked him if he was OK just for the sake of saying something. We prayed, or rather I did. I commanded the evil spirit of darkness to leave his body alone. Eze meanwhile sat there, his expressions almost wooden. It was decision time. Would taking the medication even for a few days be a case of taking several steps backward?

Eze very much needed some rest after days of no sleep. I ensured he was safely tucked into bed and then headed back to work. I silenced the lies of worries, anxiety, and so on from the enemy by choosing to congratulate myself that I had not taken an emergency afternoon off work to look after Eze but had instead left him in the care of God and His angels.

But many questions were whirling around my head. If the devil had no power, why did it seem like he had the upper hand? Tears were streaming down my face now. Not tears of defeat. Tears of frustration.

> "If there is an area of darkness in your life, then you must find the light of God's Word for that area and having done so, shine that light in that dark area!"

My pastor had said those words one Sunday. Those words had had such an impact then and played such resonance in me, I had even highlighted them in my notebook. Now those words were coming back into my spirit. Pastor had said those words for me ahead of time. They were my *rhema*—meaning a specific word for a specific person for a specific time for a specific situation.

I needed to find the light for this darkness. A key was still missing. The answer was in the Bible. That is where all the answers were. In His Word.

Eze and I had over two hundred Christian books in our collection. Nearly every week from the time we got married, there was always a fresh delivery of another book. Any book the Holy Spirit directed me to read, I bought. I spent my spare money on books rather than on clothes and shoes. Space became an issue in our already floor-to-ceiling bookshelves. Not only did I buy them, I *read* them too. I become a connoisseur of the Word. I had found many keys that had unlocked several doors till now.

We also bought as many messages from the president of our ministry. All different formats. DVDs, VCDs, audio, you name it. His voice became the other familiar voice that echoed within the walls of our house as we played his messages. I couldn't give up. Eze couldn't give up. No, not after coming this far.

Later that evening was our mid-week service at church. Our pastor always encourages that the best place for a sick person to be is not in bed but in church. Under the anointing, every yoke is broken. It was an extra long silent drive that evening as I drove Eze and myself to service.

I was very relieved to be in God's Presence, even though inside I felt frustrated and I was still wondering what the key was. Then all of a sudden, Eze made an outburst right in the middle of service. He had never done this before. He muttered something incoherent and nonsensical.

Tears were now stinging my face. In a charged atmosphere of God's Presence, how could this happen? "God, where are You?" I felt like screaming. My faith was taking a battering in the ring.

It was a bright summer evening. I remember it so clearly. I dashed out of the church. I did not know where I was going, but I felt like running. From whom, I don't know. Certainly not God, because I knew no one could run away from God, not even Jonah! (See the Book of Jonah.)

The small of my back pressed against the wall of the church boundary as I bent over trying to relieve myself of my mental anguish. Fear was taking its grip. Medication, anguish, fear...so much for my walk of faith.

"Sister Zoe?" a comforting, familiar voice said behind me. I turned. It was my pastor's wife. She had seen me make a mad dash out of the church. Hard not to notice, especially when one sits in the front pew in church, huh?

"Sister Sandra, I have had enough. I can't take anymore of this!"

Eze too had left the church and was now heading toward us. "What's the matter, honey?" his voice showing concern.

"You are the matter!" I replied, my words deliberately sounding like cut glass. "What kind of life is this?" I could now feel the anguish at the pit of my stomach. I opened my mouth as if to let it out. Only the sound of sobs came out. "In fact, you can take this!" I was handing over my wedding and engagement rings. "It's over!"

"Sister Zoe, stop that!" Sister Sandra's expression looked horrified. I had passed caring. I wanted to inflict pain on Eze. He was putting my life on hold by *allowing* this dreadful disease. Why did I have to share the burden of it? "Wear your rings please, Sister Zoe, and say you are sorry."

"Sorry!" I shot Eze a harsh look while shoving the rings back on my finger. I certainly was not sorry.

"It's your fault," Eze was telling Sister Sandra. I rolled my eyes in despair. How far gone was he? Eze never spoke to anyone like that, and certainly not to the pastor's wife!

"You see what I have to put up with, Sister Sandra!" I challenged.

"You are talking as if this will be your lot for life," she answered softly, her eyes now damp.

Thank God for my pastor's wife. As she said those words something clicked inside me. She was giving me hope. So she did not see this as the end. She was basically saying that this situation was subject to change.

"If you stick with the Word, you'll come back with a testimony!" Sister Sandra continued.

Hallelujah! That was the key. That was the light I had been searching for earlier. Now the woman of God had told me precisely what I needed. Persistence. Sticking with the Word of God against contrary conditions. Not bowing but standing firm. Like an eagle that flies toward the eye of the storm, I needed to soar right in the middle of this storm till I was above it.

They say winners never quit and quitters never win. The secret of a winner was now becoming more obvious—persistence. The key to victory. To make a further demand of faith required our persistence.

My pastor advised that Eze go back on medication, for a short while at least. Eze did and recovered very quickly, in fact in less than no time. We celebrated that victory of course, rather than focus on the fact that he had had a setback even. A quick recovery was proof positive that our faith was working and that the healing process was still in progress. The words we were hearing incessantly were giving us ascendancy. Praise God.

We stepped up even further bombardment of the Word into our spirit and soul. The messages of the president of our ministry constantly played in our house. We listened to other men and women of God too, getting more fresh revelation, building our faith block by block. Even the walls began to hear the voice of God. We went to sleep with the Word. We woke up with the Word. The pores of our flesh began to ooze God's Word.

Have Childlike Faith

Like the Canaanite woman who persisted in her faith in Matthew 15:21-28, Eze and I resolved to persist in our faith too till we got our miracle. However, in contrast to her story where she would eat the crumbs, as believers Eze knew our rights to healing as our bread. If she could get healing for her daughter when she was not entitled, how much more us?

Jesus commended the faith of this woman in the Bible. The Roman centurion was the other who Jesus commended as such. These are the only two examples in the Bible where Jesus made such a remark. Why is that? Because these two people knew they did not have rights to healing, but they were not moved by this. Of course they would have seen and/or heard of the miracles of Jesus. They had probably worked out the connection between faith and healing. So they knew faith was all they needed for their miracle.

However, whereas the Israelites knew their rights to healing as they were covenant children, these things had become too common to them. All their folks spoke about around them were stories of the Red Sea being parted, manna, Elijah and the great prophets, and so on. God had seen them through many wars victoriously. But they also knew the story of Uzzah touching the ark, of only Joshua and Caleb getting to the Promised Land, of wars they had lost due to disobedience, and so on. They were encyclopedias of information on everything that had worked for them and also against them. They knew too much. Analyst experts of every miracle and event.

The Canaanite woman and Roman centurion, on the other hand, had a childlike faith. They had not grown up with any of these testimonies. They did not know much in the area of miracles and when they worked and when they did not. They could be compared to your four-year-old whose father has promised to buy the latest toy. That four-year-old believes his dad wholeheartedly. Compare that to that same man's wife who he now promises to buy a car. She is very skeptical because she has seen all the reminder letters coming through the door of unpaid bills!

No, we must have faith in God and sift away information, statistics, and so on that will harm our faith. Forget even the negative testimonies of your experience or other Christians whom it did not seem to work for. Yes, Mr. X prayed 100 days and nights and yet nothing happened. You do not know what Mr. X really believed in his heart. No one can see anyone's heart. Mr. X could have been saying something in public yet was having a hard time believing it himself. He could have been saying another thing contrary to the right thing privately. We have all been there at one time.

We must also try not to live God's Word by our experiences. Instead, let God's Word influence our experiences. Often, many teach the Word according to their experiences, and this is where we miss it. If God's Word says black is white, then it must be so or become so. If we have not found it to be so, rather than try to explain away that particular word through our experiences and so on, we must instead ask the Holy Spirit for more revelation. The more revelation we have of God's Word the more victorious we become. There are things that we know now that Christians of many years ago did not know to enjoy. Even if you read the Bible, you will find that the revelation of God's Word progresses across the Book. Why do I say that? In the Old Testament, for example, the folks had no revelation of satan and therefore attributed disease and death to a God of vengeance and wrath. But in the New Testament we get the revelation of satan and his works. Therefore at all times, we must get more Word.

In concluding, let us remember to develop a childlike, trusting faith. As the president of my ministry says, faith never fails. If it does, he says, it was never faith.

I went back to studying material on faith. The faith of Eze and I would not fail. Oh no, not this time or ever. We were sticking with the Word and that was the end of it.

And we would be sure to come back with a testimony!

Closing Thoughts

Don't know too much of the wrong thing. Know more of the Word. Be like that four-year-old in our example. Leave the how and when to God who made the promise. It is important for you to see where you are going irrespective of what comes around you. Remain unmoved.

This means we must hold every word God tells us with all our lives. As an aside, you might be thinking, *Where do these words come from?* Most times, these words are promises from the Bible. That means if God says you are a success, even if you flunked your exams, refuse to say you are a failure.

Joseph was not a failure even as a slave in Potiphar's house.

The Lord was with Joseph, so he became a successful man. And he was in the house of his master, the Egyptian (Genesis 39:2 NASB).

That success mentality eventually spoke for Joseph in paving the way for him to become prime minister later in life.

God's Word surely cannot lie. Ever.

Summary

1. Persistence is the key to stubborn faith. Stick with the Word of God in spite of challenging circumstances.

2. If we stick with the Word of God, we will always have success. We will always come back with a testimony.

3. Have childlike faith in God. Sift away information, statistics, and so on that will harm your faith. Forget even the negative testimonies of your experience or other Christians whom it did not seem to work for.

4. The more revelation we have of God's Word the more victorious we become.

5. Faith never fails.

Confession

I refuse to give up. I refuse to give in. I am not intimidated by the devil or his cohorts. Challenges do not change my confession. I hold fast to the Word of God. As I declare God's Word, those walls are coming down. In fact, I refuse to recognize those walls of challenges. I am bold as a lion. Nothing is holding me back from getting my victory. In Jesus' name, amen.

LIFE GETS A NEW MEANING

A Godly Marriage

Eze's life was taking a new turn with each passing day. Many attributed it to the fact that he was now a happily married man. I kind of became an overnight celebrity among his friends and family as they saw the new and good changes in him.

However, while I know that I certainly helped play a key role in affecting these changes, that is not to say that someone who is not married cannot have such a testimony. Someone once said that when God wants to bless you, He brings someone into your life. Perhaps that is true of you right now. It may not necessarily be a spouse, but it may be a colleague at work for example. Always be sensitive to who God brings your way. They may contain the key to unlock that door.

Back to marriage for now. Marrying the right person is essential for a happy marital life. Next to your salvation, the most important decision you'll ever make in your life is who you marry. Marriage is not something you do because everyone else around you is doing it. I wasn't exactly a spring chicken when I walked down the aisle. Neither was Eze. We went into marriage with our eyes fully and widely opened, knowing full well that this was a contract for life.

A perfectly sane man can almost go insane if yoked to the wrong woman. A good man can be negatively influenced if married to the wrong person. Remember the story of Samson and Delilah (see Judg. 16)? Remember too, the story of Solomon, once the richest and wisest man who ever lived before Jesus, how the influence of the many wrong women he married and/or cavorted with made him more or less backslide.

Yes, we women can influence our spouses. Take note, the word is *influence*, not *manipulate*. To manipulate our husbands is akin to witchcraft. Don't be a Jezebel. Don't destroy your husband's life. A wise woman must be a *positive* influence. The Shunammite woman, for example, influenced her husband to be a blessing to the prophet Elisha (see 2 Kings 4:8-17). Yes, women are the neck, and what does the neck do? Turns the head. Not thump the head!

A foolish woman can only make her husband angry. God knew that women could have such an influence. In fact, He said, "It is not good that the man should be alone; I will make him an help meet for him" (Gen. 2:18 KJV).

Remember, we established earlier in another chapter that as a help-meet wives are the answer to their husband. This is because the husband is the vision-bearer of the family, and it is the wife's role to assist her man in achieving that vision. A helpmeet does not mean partner or supervisor. At no point did I aim to supervise Eze. I am not his mother; neither did I consider myself to be an elder sister.

Before I continue further, I wish to make the point that I am aware that this is not a book on marriage. But in some ways I cannot tell the full story without talking about the part that our marriage played in Eze's healing. In fact, the consultant psychiatrist who eventually discharged Eze acknowledged the role I had played with regard to Eze's health.

Continuing on our subject of marriage, when entering marriage neither party should go into it for what they can get from the other. Wives-to-be, take this from me—it does not matter about the car a man is driving or how much he earns. Those things are meaningless. They will not stand the test of time. Today Eze and I can have a laugh about our first date. I tease him that he could have at least valeted his car before taking out his queen-to-be on her first date. I remember sitting in his car at the time thinking this brother could have at least made an effort!

But it pays not to be fickle. What if I had decided then and there to forget the whole game and made some statement like, "Sorry mate, you seem like a nice bloke, but you are not quite what I had in mind." Trust me, I have heard such stories from guys lamenting how some women do not even give them a chance.

Money and designer clothing are not correlated to the success of marriage. If that was so, every Hollywood couple would live life happily ever after once they got hooked up. What good would it have been if Eze had turned up in a limousine and his money had been all I had been attracted to? I am clear in my mind I would have likely bolted when the going got tough.

Establish your motives for marrying. Let them be genuine. It'll save a lot of heartache later. Through all the challenges Eze and I went through brought on by mental sickness, everywhere and I mean everywhere we went people could see an unspoken bond between us. Even strangers remarked that we were well-suited. I remember one person once saying to us we were a match made in Heaven, and he had only known us five minutes! It certainly pays to be married to the right person and allow God to bring that person to you. It would help determine the quality of life you have together as a couple!

I knew Eze was very happy and content in our marriage. And I was too. Eze also helped bring out the best in me too. Through the challenges we faced, I learned something that needed my desperate attention—patience.

I had always prayed for patience. But patience is the fruit of the Spirit. It was already within me. No wonder I was not "receiving" answers. All I was required to do was draw patience out from within my recreated spirit as a born-again Christian.

But as a man of God says, patience and faith are power twins. For my faith to work, I needed to add patience. I quickly learned to apply that. I knew that now particularly, patience was required to allow God to work. Thank God for Eze; he truly showed me the meaning of being patient. Being one of the most patient people I had ever met, it was easy to imitate his exemplary example. Our marital life amidst its challenges was bliss.

Service in Church

A good marriage was just one side of the coin in Eze's life. But this was a multi-faceted coin. With the responsibilities Eze now had in church, his life definitely had a meaning. Being a worker in the house of God meant that he was relevant to the Kingdom. Our service to God is not just based on punctual attendance to church, our prayers, and our communion with Him but also on how we are propagating the Gospel. It is our duty. This is the mandate Jesus gave us before His ascension.

> *And then He told them, "Go into all the world and preach the Good News to everyone"* (Mark 16:15 NLT).

We cannot leave all the work to our pastors, preachers, and priests. We must make their work lighter by being a laborer in the house of God. We'll also spread the Gospel quicker before His coming again. Many people today still have not heard of Jesus.

When Hezekiah was at the point of death, he bargained with God to extend his life. His plea was based on his faithfulness and service to God (see 2 Kings 20:1-7). He brought God to remembrance over the many things he had done for Him. I don't believe any amount of exercising Hezekiah's faith would have resulted in turning his death sentence around, as God Himself had sent the prophet Isaiah with the news that Hezekiah would die! Imagine such a visit from a man of God.

There are times when the only way we can make a demand from God is based on the content of our plea bargain. I am sure this is what gave Hezekiah the boldness to negotiate with God. Certainly, we do not serve God for selfish motives as to what we can get in return. Our service must always come from the heart.

A great man of God in recent times needed an operation. This had been a man of God who had been faithful in his service to God over several decades, winning many to Christ and teaching God's Word tirelessly and without compromise. Being well-advanced in years, this great man did not want to go through the rigmarole of surgery. The Holy Spirit then spoke into his heart and told him it was time for him to "cash in." By this the Holy Spirit was letting him know that due to his faithfulness, God was going to perform a miracle in his body which would require him to no longer need the operation. Praise God, this was how this man of God got his healing.

Did Eze and I ever turn our face to the wall during those dark moments? Of course we did. Shortly after my dialogue with the pastor's wife that summer's evening, I turned my face to the wall. Literally and spiritually. I pleaded with God to give me the strength to carry on. I did not want to leave a man I loved and who loved me ever so much. I was getting physically tired for one thing. I reminded God of my service to Him and how much of a role Eze and I were playing in moving the Gospel.

But God renewed my strength. He gave me words of comfort in those dark moments. He told me to lean on Him. His strength was made perfect in my weakness. He would carry me on eagle's wings.

The president of the ministry our church belongs to always emphasizes that the work we do in church is the most important work we do in life, even above our careers and jobs. Many Christians don't see working in the house of God as something relevant or a force to be reckoned with. But know this—nothing in our service to God can ever be considered insignificant.

Getting Rid of Distractions

Eze loved watching "Star Trek" when I met him. He boasted of being a great fan, knew all the characters, and watched most of the episodes. Most evenings, he spent hours as a couch potato flicking channels.

I am not against entertainment or television viewing, but I do believe there is a time for everything. There is also the proportion of time to consider in indulging our flesh. The more you grow in the things of the spirit, the less the things of the world mean to you. We must always choose God unreservedly.

> *Stop loving the world and the things that are in the world. If anyone persists in loving the world, the Father's love is not in him* (1 John 2:15 ISV).

Be wary of what you say you "love." The Bible is specific on what or who we should love. Don't be carried away with the use of that word. Your use of the word may be a pointer of something you need to address in relation to James 4:4.

Anyway, with Eze I also believed that when there are issues to be sorted out, time becomes a very expensive commodity. There had been many wasted years in his life. In fact, someone had cheekily asked him shortly before I met him what he had to show for his brains and his age. If Eze was not stirred in his spirit by such a statement, well I was when he recounted it to me! If God was to restore those years, it would not be via "Star Trek". Television was not the solution, especially if our spirits were not being edified or built up.

You see, many people complain of their several problems but are not prepared to put in the time and/or sacrifice to change their situation.

There was a lot of garbage in Eze's life that mental illness had brought that needed to be thrown out. I have already spelled a lot of these out to you in previous chapters. I did not need a degree to know that Eze was definitely living far below his potential. But here's a secret. In a new relationship, men are often trying to please or impress the one they are courting. My personal view is that now is the best time to develop good habits together.

In our case, Eze and I did just that. We started doing Bible study together and we also became prayer partners. It kept us out of mischief and also provided a solid foundation for our marriage. The good thing was that Eze soon found that he lost interest in television, as he was enjoying the fellowship we were sharing together with the Holy Spirit. This does prove that communion with the Holy Spirit is sweet and has the power to wean off any television addict. That's the anointing of the Holy Spirit.

Eze also became less of a social addict, always having to be at some social meeting or outing. After we got married, we spent so much time doing the Lord's work and studying the Word that neither of us had time left for social events and activities. Eze also found that he was managing his time better because his time became of more value to him. I could see that nothing was detracting Eze from his goal toward his healing. There was a fire, a passion in him now burning with his soul. We were making so many sacrifices in the name of the Gospel.

> *"Yes," Jesus replied, "and I assure you that everyone who has given up house or wife or brothers or parents or children, for the sake of the Kingdom of God, will be repaid many times over in this life, and will have eternal life in the world to come"* (Luke 18:29-30 NLT).

Don't be afraid to make sacrifices along the way. There are heavenly rewards for your service to God, but there are also earthly ones too. Yes, one of Eze's first payments has indeed been his healing. And there is surely more to come.

With the work of Holy Spirit having free will to work in Eze's life instead of Eze being in some imaginary space clouds of "Star Trek", Eze was also getting to learn how to be in tune with the Holy Spirit and to hear from God.

When you want changes in your life, you must hear from God. Does God still speak today? Emphatically yes. However, we must train our spiritual ears if we wish to hear from Him. If your radio is not switched on, it doesn't mean that there is no broadcast. To get a broadcast, we must tune in to the Holy Spirit. We need to get rid of the distractions—the static noise that makes it difficult to hear.

> *My sheep hear My voice, and I know them, and they follow Me* (John 10:27 NASB).

What a better life it is for the sheep when they follow their Shepherd. Think about the many pitfalls they avoid and the wolves that are driven away, far from the sheep. The Shepherd loves His sheep and is very protective over them.

Isn't Jesus wonderful?

Closing Thoughts

When you become a born-again Christian your life *must* change. If it does not, then you need to speak to your pastor or priest. I am not saying that you may necessarily experience a radical change the minute you accept Jesus as your Lord and Savior, although that can happen, but you must know you are now embarking on a new journey.

That new journey was what changed the apostle Paul from being a mass murderer to Christ's bondservant. If medicine can have an effect on our bodies, how much more something as potent and powerful as the power of God in our lives? But this Christian life must never be static.

Most human beings do resent change. There are even courses that teach people how to manage change. But the only constant in life is change. So when change comes as the Holy Spirit starts directing your life, go with the flow. Don't go against the currents of God.

Eze got more than he bargained for when he married me. I say that jokingly, but in many ways that is true. Marriage, as we have established, must bring out the best in each person. I am not advocating that marriage does not come without its challenges. What good thing from God doesn't? But admit it or not, marriage will change you. Yes, I also got a good side of the bargain in more ways than I can count. Of course, marrying someone diagnosed with a serious disorder such as mental illness comes with its own agenda. However, trust me, if it is not mental illness it will be something else. All in all, how it comes only makes the union sweeter and more cherishable.

Other radical changes that we have to face up to in our Christian walk is that often times, many Christians will lose friends along the way. This is rather unfortunate but sometimes a necessary thing, especially if your lives and values are going in opposite directions. We have to flee temptations as the Bible admonishes, and sometimes old friends can lure us back into lifestyles and values we have laid at the altar. It is important that your friends understand the new you and support you.

Yes, life requires blunt decisions at times if you will walk in the paths that God has laid for you. Yes, while we still pray for old friends, God may require that some friendships are severed. It does not even have to be that the other person is necessarily bad or not a Christian. Paul and Barnabas went their separate ways after a while and each did mighty things for God.

Life taking on a new meaning also means living the lesser for the greater. As we saw with Eze, he gave up his "Star Trek" viewing for greater things. There's no sin in watching a decent television show, but there was work to be done. The pleasures of those things took less precedence as God's work and service took more prominence.

All these are just examples of what it means when we make Jesus *Lord* of our lives. It means our lives are no longer our own. If you want His lordship with all the benefits, submit to Him. As you do I can sincerely promise you that you will enjoy life even more. No, enjoy your recreation now and again, but let Jesus be Lord!

Summary

1. Marrying the right person is essential for a happy marital life. Next to your salvation, the most important decision you'll

ever make in your life is who you marry. Don't be unequally yoked in marriage.

2. Being a worker in the house of God makes you relevant to the Kingdom of God. The work we do in church is the most important work we do in life, even above our careers and jobs. Many Christians don't see working in the house of God as something relevant or a force to be reckoned with. Nothing in our service to God can ever be considered insignificant. There are heavenly rewards for your service to God, but there are also earthly ones too.

3. Many people complain of their several problems but are not prepared to put in the time and/or sacrifice to change their situation. Distractions are just one of such things. We must even be prepared to rid ourselves of anything that steals our time from being effective in getting the answers we so desire from God.

4. When you want changes in your life, you must hear from God. We must train our ears to hear from God so we get clear direction for our lives. This is the way to guaranteed success.

Prayer

Thank You Lord that my life has now taken on a new meaning in Christ. Thank You for all the promises that this new life brings. Thanks for my wonderful spouse. Help me, Lord, to appreciate him or her at all times, no matter what. Thank You for the opportunity to serve You. Help me to be found a good and faithful servant on that day. Direct me, Lord, in establishing the right connections with the right people. Help me to deal with any distraction that takes away my focus and attention from You. Thank You that You are Lord of my life. I rest in that knowledge, knowing that I have the best that life can offer me because of that. In Jesus' name, amen.

TAKING CARE OF OUR BODIES AS TEMPLES OF THE HOLY SPIRIT

Handling Stress

A bridge, for example, is designed to cope with levels of pressure and tension. If this level is exceeded, the bridge is at risk of collapse or damage. Is your body at risk of collapse due to stress?

There is an old adage that says, "I am too blessed to be stressed." In reality, I do believe that we are designed to cope with a certain level of stress. Most times, most people who say they are stressed usually feel stressed.

Our bodies can cope with tensions and pressures of life. Even everyday and mundane tasks can be stressors. Do you know some people can get flustered just by thinking of what to put on or what to eat? How about the stresses of increased gas prices? These stressors most times get us more upset than tipping over the edge. Yes, we endure most things without feeling stressed.

But then yes, real tensions do come in life. Everyday stressors can mount up. But we established earlier that challenges for a Christian are for our promotion. The so-called pressures brought on by our challenges should by no means destroy us. We are meant to be eagles that fly right into the center of a raging storm. We go right into the war zone, and as God intends we should come out unscathed.

What we have to train ourselves to do is always—no matter how big or small—rely on God's strength instead of our human strength. That way we can avoid pushing ourselves beyond our limits. Why? Because we have a limitless God. And if we do push ourselves beyond our capacity, the supernatural power and strength of God should kick in like a standby generator to see us through! When that strength envelopes us, we will feel refreshed and revived. That strength multiplies our human strength. We become super beings. Your ability is of God. Remember Paul's mentality. He confessed he could do all things through Christ who strengthened him. Imagine how we would just coast through life with such a mindset.

Mentally first decide to put *everything, absolutely everything,* in His care. Doing so will help you go a long way in ensuring you stay in good health physically and mentally. Remember God has the aerial view of your life. He knows the end from the beginning.

In avoiding stress we can go a long way in steering clear of an over-worked mind. What do I mean? Trying to figure out everything. Don't allow your thoughts to run loose. Guard them. Think about what you are thinking about. We have already gone through some of these points earlier, but they are worth mentioning again to emphasize the points. We must guard our imaginations. Don't dwell on the wrong imaginations till *you* make them become a reality by acting them out and giving place to the devil. Such mental stress can bring on attacks of depression, psychosis, and a whole host of mental ailments, so avoid them!

Another vital point in our subject of stress is paying close attention to what you hear. We have already touched on this, but again this cannot be overemphasized. Instead of listening to rumors of downsizing at work, which more than likely may cause your heart to start racing, why don't you listen to the good sermons and uplifting messages instead?

Following on from what we hear, *watch what you watch.* The world will show you the documentaries on the poor statistics of this and that. How does that help you in your faith walk? You need to decide where you stand. Are you going to believe God's Word for your healing, prosperity, and so on, or would you rather the experts share their doom and gloom on how hopeless things are? Experts themselves are still learning. So sieve out information that is not going to help you move forward. The world does not often move in the same direction as the Word of God. Watch the voice of the world and risk getting the wrong idea of what is right. If you want to live free and stress free too, know the Truth.

Also, hang out with the right people. People who encourage rather than criticize. People who can pray together with you and talk about God rather than people who just add more coal to your burning anxieties.

Avoid people who gossip and all forms of evil communication. If your communication with a particular person always leaves you reeling, it is about time you thought seriously about laying that friendship on the altar. You may be surprised how much "saner" you feel afterward when you make a decision to remove yourself from such people! Find friends who add and multiply rather than subtract and divide.

The topic of stress is huge, but I would also like to draw on a very important point here. It is worth noting that *sometimes* eliminating huge levels of stress in our lives can be achieved by staying in the will of God for our lives. I use the word sometimes cautiously, as we all know how Jesus sweated blood in the Garden of Gethsemane at the thought of what He had to do, which was the will of the Father. It is no secret that Jesus was in great anguish. The medical condition for sweating blood is actually called *hematohidrosis*. This is linked to extreme stress which causes the blood vessels around the sweat glands to rupture. Yet having said that, going against the will of God can cause us to go in the wrong direction for our lives. This will never help matters in life. So stay in God's will and you will be in the safest place in the world even when the storms come, and you know you will win in the end as Jesus did in spite of His drama in the Garden!

Adopt a Healthy Lifestyle

Sometimes people lose their healing simply because they go back to their old lifestyles. Old lifestyles can include unhealthy living such as bad diet and lack of exercise to name two. Although Jesus said that we do not live by bread alone but by the Word of God, that does not form the grounds for careless eating.

I already mentioned that when I met Eze I did my best to help along with ensuring he had a balanced diet. Yes, by all means we are called to live the supernatural life. But that supernatural life does not equate to abuse. Jesus Himself had a healthy diet. He ate fish on several occasions, for example, but would have eaten lamb and poultry too. His diet also contained lots of whole grain foods, bread, vegetables, and legumes. Jesus practiced what He preached. He took care of His body. He set the standard. And remember that though He was God, He lived as a man. At times, He felt hungry like the rest of us and He felt tired just like us too.

Our bodies are the temples of the Holy Spirit. The Holy Spirit actually lives inside every Christian. In the Old Testament, the Holy Spirit dwelt in tents and then buildings. This was the temple. There were prescribed rules and regulations in which the physical temple of God had to be kept holy and sanctified. There were chambers in the temple that only certain people were allowed to enter. Failure to adhere to any of these laws could result in death!

How different is that consequence today? If the people in the Old Testament risked losing their lives for defiling the temple, we may also run the same risks with our bodies today. To constantly have a fast food diet day in, day out for several years is certainly not recommended for your health. Not getting enough sleep will eventually take its toll. A lack of the right nutrients can cause lack of concentration. Abusing your body through the use of illicit drugs, smoking, excessive alcohol, and so on eventually damages your health in one way or the other. Our bodies were not designed for this maltreatment.

Elijah was depressed, probably exhausted and worn out after defeating the prophets.

> *Elijah was afraid and ran for his life. When he came to Beersheba in Judah, he left his servant there, while he himself went a day's journey into the desert. He came to a broom tree, sat down under it and prayed that he might die. "I have had enough, Lord," he said. "Take my life; I am no better than my ancestors." Then he lay down under the tree and fell asleep. All at once an angel touched him and said, "Get up and eat." He looked around, and there by his head was a cake of bread baked over hot coals, and a jar of water. He ate and drank and then lay down again. The angel of the Lord came back a second time and touched him and said, "Get up and eat, for the journey is too much for you." So he got up and ate and drank. Strengthened by that food, he traveled forty days and forty nights until he reached Horeb, the mountain of God. There he went into a cave and spent the night...* (1 Kings 19:3-9).

God sent an angel to provide Elijah with food and drink. The angel gave Elijah the most ordinary and practical advice. Twice the angel gave Elijah food to eat. God was ensuring Elijah was eating regularly. In verse 7, it actually says Elijah was strengthened by the food provided. No prayer was involved here. In fact, so strengthened was Elijah that he traveled forty days and forty nights. This is not the same as comfort food. Make no mistake. Some people turn to food as their comfort when they feel low. This is sometimes called emotional eating. Emotional eating is where food is used as a distraction from the challenges one is facing. Remember that the Word of God is the one and only true comfort food that can help anyone out of depression without the dangers of getting overweight or obese!

In the story told in First Kings, we can see that Elijah also rested. The angel did not tell him to do so, but at least Elijah had the good sense to do so. Rest is not akin to being idle. His body certainly felt rejuvenated afterward. A good rest and meal can certainly help with getting you out of feelings of being low. A good rest recharges a clogged mind. We do read accounts that Jesus slept too (see Mark 4:38).

After we got married, I ensured through my cooking and food shopping that Eze's diet was varied and had all the right nutrients. One of the side effects of the medication during the times he was taking it was high cholesterol. Practical habits such as a low-fat diet, cutting down on red meat while trimming the fat, removing poultry skin, eating lots of fish, and cooking with olive or grapeseed oil are some of what our diet consisted of and consists of still. Coupled with prayer, Eze's cholesterol level quickly reduced without the need of any cholesterol-lowering tablets.

Eze was also concerned about his weight. Once again, medication had caused him to put on artificial weight. I encouraged Eze to always start the day with a good breakfast. Studies have shown that people who eat breakfast are slimmer than those who do not. The reason that is often cited is that those who do not eat breakfast put their bodies on alert meaning their metabolism slows down. The body then clings onto any food, particularly any fat eaten afterward. A good start with breakfast in your day gives your metabolism a kick start. I have maintained the same dress size so far for all of my adult life to date, no matter the portions I eat, by just employing this principle. This is my secret!

For Eze, having a good breakfast also kept him alert. Trying to combat the drowsiness of the drugs was one thing, but a hearty bowl of porridge in the mornings (porridge is low in fat and sugars) was half the battle won.

The Debate of Supplements and Medicine

Some Christians debate if it is wrong to take supplements. Let's not over-spiritualize the things of God. God is not averse to medicine. Satan does not want you well, so why would he give doctors and scientists wisdom to make you better? Think about it. The wisdom is from Almighty God! That is why it is good to pray for increased wisdom for people in medical and pharmaceutical companies. Taking food supplements, especially multivitamins and mineral supplements, does not mean you are not walking in faith. Neither does taking medication mean that you lack faith or are a weak Christian or a less mature Christian. The priests were given medical instructions in the Old Testament. People were healed by medicine in the Bible. Hezekiah was healed by a poultice of figs. Luke was a doctor. How did he cure his patients?

It is in fact wise to take supplements, especially if our diets are lacking in vital nutrients as is often the case these days. Current scientific research has shown that vitamin B is of great benefit in alleviating stress, fatigue, and lethargy. Also vitamin B12 deficiency has also been shown to cause mania and psychosis. Vitamin B is often called the stress vitamin. In fact, a diet deficient in vitamin B makes one more prone to stress and anxiety! Taking a vitamin B complex supplement can go a long way in maintaining good mental health. So consider getting this supplement, especially if your stress is due to deficiency in your diet.

Worth mentioning is good old cod liver oil! Many children grew up taking a teaspoon of that liquid oily stuff every morning. Argh! How could the pharmaceutical companies have made such a thing? On a more serious note, Eze found that cod liver oil also went a long way in improving his mental thinking and alertness, especially when he started reducing his medication. Cod liver oil is said to help with brain function activity and also to alleviate stress. Fish oils too and many other supplements can really maintain a good mental and physical health. Of course, discuss any supplements you take with your physician, especially if you are on any medication.

Delegate Responsibilities

Sharing responsibilities also assists your mental health. Jethro, Moses' father-in-law, was very concerned about Moses' workload (see Exod. 18:13-23). Moses was taking on all the responsibilities. This was unnecessary. He actually told Moses:

What you are doing is not good. You and these people who come to you will only wear yourselves out. The work is too heavy for you; you cannot handle it alone (Exodus 18:17-18).

In Eze's case, he married me, which meant we could now share responsibilities and help each other out in certain issues. That plus being in a church where the brethren were very helpful certainly meant he could call on a brother or sister in Christ when in need of any help. Perhaps you are not married, but that is the benefit of being in a good church. Enlist the help of your brethren in Christ, especially if the load gets to be too much. Yes, we can do all things through Christ who strengthens and in time can take up more challenges, but while you are growing in the things of God, don't be too shy to ask for help.

Closing Thoughts

Stress is a common word these days. Stress is often a trigger for several mental disorders and today is linked to many physical ailments. People are desperate for release. God seriously cares about our well-being. He does not want you burned out! In fact, He tells us to labor to enter the rest of God (see Heb. 4:11). The word *labor* actually means to be diligent, make haste, and make every effort. That is how serious God is about us avoiding stress!

Praying cannot be overlooked in moments of stress. Prayer is important. Praying in tongues also puts you on a level above. As we do so, we are emboldened and strengthened. This was Paul's secret of success. He said he prayed in tongues more than everyone (see 1 Cor. 14:18). Yes, develop your prayer language. Speak more in tongues than in your understanding, and you will make strides.

Interestingly, Dr. Carl Peterson, a psychiatrist of Oral Roberts University, did a research linking speaking in tongues with our immunity. He discovered that as we speak in tongues an activity begins in the brain that releases two chemical secretions, giving a 35-40 percent boost in the immune system. This, he said, aided healing within our bodies. What was interesting about his research was that the secretions were triggered from a part of the brain that we don't use and that has no other apparent activity in humans.

I personally believe after reading the research that God designed us to speak in tongues so we could get the release of these secretions to heal our bodies. This is certainly worth thinking about.

Finally, John says:

> *...I came that they may have and enjoy life, and have it in abundance (to the full, till it overflows)* (John 10:10 AMP).

A life that overflows is not one weighed down with anxiety, mental stress, and sickness. Let us ensure, where common sense prevails, we make use of it and not be reckless about the life God has given us.

Summary

1. Control the amount of stress in your life. Mentally first decide to put everything, absolutely everything, in His care. Don't try to figure out everything.

2. Don't allow your thoughts to run loose. Guard them. Think about what you are thinking about. We must guard our imaginations. Don't dwell on the wrong imaginations till you make them become a reality by acting them out and giving place to the devil.

3. Hang out with the right people. People who encourage rather than criticize. People who can pray together with you and talk about God.

4. Adopting a healthy lifestyle goes a long way. Eating well, exercising, getting enough rest, and taking food supplements are important ingredients in maintaining a good lifestyle.

5. Learn to delegate responsibilities.

Confession

My body is the temple of the Holy Ghost. I therefore take good care of my body at all times. I refuse sickness and disease to come into this body. I speak divine health into my body from the crown of my head to the soles of my feet. In Jesus' name, amen.

Chapter Twelve ─────────────────────────────

THE END OF THE ROAD

Soon after Eze had the last episode I spoke about earlier—the one where he had made an out-of-character outburst in church—he quickly came off the medication once again. In fact, he was only on it for a few days, possibly about three or four days in total. This was a major feat, considering that when we started exercising our faith he would stay on medication for a few weeks or so after an episode before weaning himself off it again.

Though he was off the medication after this last attack, Eze was still feeling very stressed by changes in work, meaning the trigger of the attack was very much still present. But by not taking the medication, we were now taking a new leap of faith here. Usually Eze would have stayed on the drugs if he was still feeling stressed. Make no mistake here—he was certainly not back to his normal self. But remember what I said earlier. Following my conversation with my pastor's wife, I had discovered the next and what was to be the final key. The key of persistence. Persisting on the Word and on our rights.

Things were definitely not rosy. In fact, Eze was again slipping back into another attack. And the symptoms were coming on full and strong. But then I remembered a powerful testimony that had been given in church. That testimony was to mark the end of our journey in the world of psychiatry. Thank God for the sharing of testimonies!

The Final Step

A brother in our church had been four hours away from death, according to the reports of his doctors to his family. He had suffered a massive stroke and was basically lying in a coma in the hospital. There was not much the doctors could do except count down his remaining hours. His family members were told to prepare themselves for the inevitable.

However, two hours into the brother's life sentence, the wife noticed that her husband's lips were moving. The brother was saying something. On close examination, he was actually praying in the spirit, in tongues. But he was still unconscious in a coma. However, something supernatural began to happen. As he lay praying, his body started responding, and not too long after he woke from his coma and, as they say, lived to tell the tale.

Now with Eze slipping back into the familiar evil mental world again, I spoke to him. I had determined to myself that if a half-dead man could bring himself back to life, then even a semi-conscious man or anyone not in control of his or her full senses could bring about the change the person required. Another leap of faith.

Staring into Eze's half-dazed eyes, I told him to command the demons troubling him to let him go. I knew within myself that if Eze's healing was to be permanent, Eze had to independently reach the point of convincement with regard to his healing and therefore take it by force. Everyone had prayed for him to date, and yes of course he had gotten this far through those prayers. Yes, God had met Eze's need for healing at a lower level, where everyone was exercising faith for Eze on his behalf. It was now time for Eze to take this final step. The devil's time with this was up.

After all, it was Hezekiah who had turned his face to the wall. It was Hezekiah who had wept sore. It was Hezekiah who had pleaded his case. I had carried Eze on my faith. Our pastor had carried Eze on his faith. Everyone had carried Eze on their faith. Yes, hands had been laid. These were all the reasons he had even got this far. Praise God that our prayers can cause a change in someone else's life. But often in maintaining a permanent healing, you have to have knowledge of God's Word for yourself. You have to develop your own faith. You have to have your own prayer life: Someone else's faith is not enough to resist the enemy's attacks. No one prayed for Hezekiah as far as we know. Isaiah did not. No, the man of God certainly did not pray for him (see Isa. 38:1-3).

Make no mistake, when you are walking in faith—and oftentimes it is when you are almost at your final destination—the enemy will test you without relent. Someone once said when the enemy is leaving he makes a loud noise. The devil is the number one attention seeker. He seems increasingly merciless at those times. But when you *resist the devil, he will flee* (see James 4:7).

Thank God, Eze responded to what I said. In a stern voice, Eze commanded satan to leave his body in the name of Jesus and never to return. "In the name of Jesus, I command you to leave my body and never return again!" he said. Eze took his rightful stand. He was enforcing life.

Well, nothing tangible happened immediately when Eze spoke, but I knew this was now the end. Sometimes, we may feel something when we are ministered to or when we speak authoritatively. We may shriek, shout, scream, fall to the ground, or even feel heat or cold. But not so this time with Eze. Don't always look for a tangible sign. Just speak with faith and believe.

Eze indeed had spoken with such authority. And the words had come from within *his* spirit. I knew he had won. He had the medal of victory. Even at this point I knew he did not need a doctor's report to verify his healing. The note of victory was reverberating at full volume.

Yes, the devil fled that day, probably with his tail between his legs. Eze walked free that day and has never looked back again. If you stick with the Word, you'll come back with a testimony indeed!

Closing Thoughts

The devil will challenge you every step of the way, even at the last step. We must remember, however, that the battle has already been won. Remember, Jesus defeated him over two thousand years ago. Those little demons that seek to torment you saw their master boss, satan, paraded in shame and defeat. Always remember that whenever you think that satan has gotten too big in your life. That is a lie.

As Christians it also helps when we look at things and play our lives backward. What do I mean? The Word of God tells us we are healed, for example. But right now your body is racked with sickness and disease. If we keep the picture—the perspective that God has said we have won over this sickness—then we can be more relaxed about how we handle the challenges of that poor health condition. While others are fretting, you remain rested because you have a secret. You know you have the victory even though in the physical it looks quite the opposite.

We each get to a level in our Christian walk where we take accountability, just as a child grows up and becomes more responsible. As we make those bold strides forward, the devil has to start thinking of new tactics to come against you. And that is where you have the advantage. The devil has no imagination. There are no new tricks where he is concerned. He always comes with the same games. Knowing this means you can stay ahead of his game.

As we resist the devil, he will certainly flee. We must stand bold and strong and not shake. The struggle is over. Don't nail Jesus again on the Cross. Refuse to struggle. Refuse to be frightened of the devil. Never be perturbed, even if the devil showed up in all his gear in front of your naked eyes. Enter God's rest. Remember the Word says *behold*, we have been given power (the right word is authority) to tread on serpents and scorpions (see Luke 10:19 NKJV). *Behold* in that verse tells us to take particular note, by the way! Those serpents and scorpions are the devil and his little demons. Also that verse also says that *nothing* shall by any means harm us.

You have a sure victory!

Summary

1. Persist on the Word and your rights in Christ.

2. We must take ownership eventually in our Christian walk. This we do by continuing to grow in the things of God.

3. Stand in authority of who you are. As you resist satan, he will flee—with his tail between his legs too!

Confession

I have the victory, hallelujah! Nothing shall by any means harm me because the devil has been defeated. Nothing shall by any means harm me. As I resist the devil and his cohorts with the Word of God, he flees. I am not afraid of the devil. He is a defeated foe. In Jesus' name, amen.

THE IMPORTANCE OF TESTIMONIES

Jesus wants everyone to tell others their testimony. He wants people to share what God has done. To let others know that we are free from the clutches of the enemy and help others in their faith too. Ultimately, God wants us to *hold fast that which is good*, including healing (see 1 Thess. 5:21).

Why People Don't Share Testimonies

Many people are scared to give testimonies. In fact, some Christians encourage others not to share their testimonies publicly. A lot of people feel that by sharing their testimonies, they may be perceived as showing off. My response to that is, "Why not?" Hang on. We must show off what *God* has done, not to put ourselves on pedestals or draw attention to ourselves but to encourage others. It is only the devil who can whisper lies to you that by sharing your testimony, you are on an ego trip. It is *not* an act of humility when you do not share your testimonies. It can even be perceived as an act of selfishness. How do we reach the souls of the lost or fainthearted if we do not share with them the goodness of God?

Some think that sharing their testimonies breeds envy. The problem in that case does not lie with you but with the listener's own insecurities. Jesus was certainly not affected by the Pharisees and Sadducees. In spite of their obvious envy and jealousy, Jesus kept His focus. Why don't you too?

Maybe you are thinking that your testimony is not extraordinary or dramatic enough to be told. Jesus' first miracle was not raising a dead man, Lazarus, who had been dead for three days. Even the first person He raised from the dead was Jairus' daughter who had just died (see

Luke 8:49). Jesus Himself worked His faith. He grew His faith. As He did so, so did the "complexities" of the miracles He performed. You have to start somewhere. When Eze started sharing his testimony of the changes in his life, they were not anything perceived as wonderfully spectacular. But he started from somewhere till he got to the spectacular. Praise God!

Another reason why I believe people don't share their testimonies is that they believe perhaps that the devil on hearing them share their testimonies and will bring back the problem or even give them fresh ones. They don't want the devil to hear them glorifying God for their healing. The point is the devil is on the lookout to steal what God has given you. Isn't he a thief?

But don't be fooled by that old trickster, the devil. He is your enemy, not your friend. He never takes sides with you. He does not care about your interests. As I mentioned earlier, he is certainly not going to congratulate you for your healing. He may even try to put symptoms back on you. The reason for this is because he wants you ill again so others will doubt the power of God. By maintaining your healing, many will be caused to believe in divine healing and satan certainly does not want this. He would rather people perished in ignorance. But if you know your rights, you'll soon get him speeding off from you rather than you trying to hide from him.

You need to call the devil's bluff. Revelation 12:11 confirms that one way to overcome the devil is certainly by the word of our testimonies. The devil hates the sharing of testimonies. Why? Because as Revelation 12:11 says, we overcome him when we do.

The Facts of Mental Illness

Before we delve further into the importance of testimonies, let us consider a few facts to understand the impact that when we get healed, God *must* be glorified:

- The dictionary defines mental illness as: Any of various conditions characterized by impairment of an individual's normal cognitive, emotional, or behavioral functioning, and caused by social, psychological, biochemical, genetic, or other factors, such as infection or head trauma. Also called emotional illness, mental disease, mental disorder.

- Mental illness is a very broad field and one that is often hard to diagnose accurately. Cultural, personal, religious, and social factors can often lead to wrong diagnosis. It is often perceived that those with mental problems have issues with alcohol and drug abuse. This may indeed be so, but was not the case with Eze, who is 100 percent a teetotaler and has never even touched any drug substance.

- Mental disorders include anxiety disorders, psychosis, personality disorders, eating disorders—the list goes on and on. Schizophrenia is often described as psychosis and is one of the most debilitating mental illnesses. Symptoms usually include hearing voices and seeing things which others do not. Often sufferers cannot distinguish thoughts from reality. They may become withdrawn and unable to concentrate.

- People suffering from schizophrenia usually have higher IQs.

- Employers discriminate against people with mental disorders, often leading to high unemployment rates among them. This subsequently often leads to homelessness, especially among those suffering from psychosis who have to cope with a crowd of confusing thoughts.

- Mental health professionals are often reluctant to assist sufferers in coming off medication. Withdrawal effects can often mirror psychiatric symptoms to include depression, mania, and hallucinations.

However, in all of the above, all things, including complete healing, are possible with God!

Share the Full Testimony

We have got to tell all. This is what grabs my attention with the woman with the issue of blood. She wanted to escape unnoticed. But Jesus had other plans. He wanted the person who had drawn virtue from Him to come forward and have the opportunity to proclaim what had happened, because something was in store for them. It was her day. Is today your day? Jesus knew that by coming forward, she stood to gain more than healing.

Praise God, the woman came forward. She went from divine healing to divine health. That day she was made whole.

> *Then the woman, seeing that she could not go unnoticed, came trembling and fell at His feet. In the presence of all the people, she told why she had touched Him and how she had been instantly healed* (Luke 8:47).

Jesus had asked who touched Him when He felt virtue—that is power—come out of Him as this woman had been healed. Do you not think Jesus knew who had really touched Him? He had a reason for His question. He wanted her to come forward and testify. And see, she came forward even though she was trembling and gave her account in the presence of *all* the people. She did not go home and tell her immediate family. No sneaking away that day. No, the whole crowd heard. There could be no going back. Everyone heard her testimony that day, and many are still hearing her testimony today.

In Mark 5:33, we also learn that the woman told Jesus *all* the truth. Not half truths or missing puzzles. Not what she thought may have happened either. You have to realize this woman had a so-called disgraceful situation. Her friends would have shunned her because of her condition. Her coming out even meant risking her life. She had been used to the so-called secret life as she was forbidden to go anywhere in public. This is the plight of this woman we are talking about. But this woman did not hold back on the truth.

Dangers of Being Economical With Your Testimony

I once heard a testimony from the president of the ministry we belong to of how a man had been in one of the ministry's healing crusades. The man in question came forward to be ministered to after feeling the power of God go through his body. When the man of God asked him to share his testimony, the man said he had been suffering from leukemia. The man of God, however, felt within his spirit that this was a fabricated truth and challenged the man on this, giving him the opportunity to correct his half-truths. The man then whispered that in fact he was an HIV patient but did not want his friends and family to know what he had been suffering from. The man of God cautioned him that he must look beyond that and on receiving his healing he must tell people the truth of his HIV suffering. But pride got in the man's way and he did not do as he had been instructed. Not very long after, the man did in fact die.

How sad. How very sad. The man had a ticket to keep his healing but allowed another tool of the enemy, pride, to prevent him from receiving his blessing. He did not tell all, and as a consequence lost his life.

The stigma of HIV stood between this man and his life. I have already touched on stigmas in another chapter. I pointed out that we must not classify the devil's works for him. He likes no one. His works are his works whether you feel a headache or are diagnosed with HIV. Which would you prefer anyway, to be labeled or even laughed at or to be alive? Think about it. Don't let stigma prevent you from getting what belongs to you. Don't respond either to any mental challenges by being in denial. Denial is often a way of trying to protect our reputation or image. The long and short of it all is that denial amounts to pride. Remember, God resists the proud; "God opposes the proud but gives grace to the humble" (1 Peter 5:5). You want God on your side, not opposed to you. The humble are exalted. They receive grace. Take your stand and tell *all*. That way you keep your healing and are made whole!

> *And He said unto her, Daughter, be of good comfort: thy faith hath made thee whole; go in peace* (Luke 8:48 KJV).

That was another reason Jesus wanted the woman with the issue of blood to share her testimony. There are divine laws. She had received her healing by divine means. She needed to keep her healing by divine means or she stood the risk of losing it. Notice how Jesus called her "daughter" too. This let the woman know that she had now resumed her place in society. There is no more so-called stigma. She got her self-esteem and dignity back that day.

Why We Decided to Share

Eze and I are not ashamed to tell of what God has done in our lives with his healing. That way faith can rise up in people who are in a similar or desperate situation. I did some research while writing this book. Here are some startling statistics:

- An estimated 26.2 percent of Americans age 18 and older—about one in four adults—suffer from a diagnosable mental disorder in a given year. (National Institute of Mental Health)

- Many people suffer from more than one mental disorder at a time. (National Institute of Mental Health)

- About 2.4 million Americans—1.1 percent of the population—are diagnosed with schizophrenia. (National Institute of Mental Health)

- About 450 million people worldwide have a mental health problem. (World Health Organization 2001)

The devil does not even show mercy to children:

- One in ten children between the ages of one and 15 has a mental health disorder in the UK. (The Office for National Statistics, Great Britain)

Just look at those figures above, especially the World Health Organization figures of 450 million people. There is no reason for needless suffering. How can we keep silent of God's power and goodness with that many people worldwide, even children, suffering with a mental health problem? Scientifically, to date the cause of schizophrenia, for example, has not been determined. Just like many diseases, there are times when doctors can offer no cure. At best, they can treat the symptoms. While we applaud medical workers, God always has a cure. God does not say it is over unless you do. God never gives up on anyone. For Eze and I that means there are 450 million people or their families who need to hear our story! That is 450 million people who can be offered hope that they can have a normal life as God intended. But how do 450 million get to hear this story?

Back to our discussion, people get to hear of God's goodness only through our testimonies. We must never tire of proclaiming the good news package, healing being part of it.

As Jesus was getting into the boat, the man who had been demon-possessed begged to go with him. Jesus did not let him, but said, "Go home to your family and tell them how much the Lord has done for you, and how He has had mercy on you." So the man

138

went away and began to tell in the Decapolis how much Jesus had done for him. And all the people were amazed (Mark 5:18-20).

Jesus told the demon-possessed man of the Gerasenes to go home and tell his family. He wanted the man's family to hear how much the Lord had done—the good news. But the man went over and above that instruction. He went to the Decapolis, which is in fact ten cities. The demon-possessed man became a missionary. A man who once had a stigma, a social outcast who once lived in tombs, was now a preacher and evangelist. People were amazed. He had a dramatic story to tell. The ex-demoniac had experienced a dramatic change. I am sure many believed and sought Jesus too for themselves. In fact, when Jesus visited the Decapolis later, they sought after Him to heal their sick. Jesus had to even take the deaf and dumb man away from the crowd to perform a miracle. The people's hearts were ripe to receive their miracles. They had heard how much the Lord had done. Faith had come and had come by hearing.

The Sunday after the consultant psychiatrist signed Eze off indefinitely, Eze and I mounted the pulpit in our church to share the glorious and final chapter of our testimony. All along we had shared with the brethren every stage of progress. Now the medical team had finally agreed with the heavenly team.

Many in the congregation told me afterward that tears were streaming as Eze and I recounted all. The steps we had taken, the setbacks, and our final victory. Yes, we were more than conquerors. We were overcomers.

Always rejoice when others give testimonies. Never be envious, thinking, "Why not me?" when you hear the glory of God in another's life. Instead, hearing testimonies should propel your faith to receive your miracle. Never ask when either. Even when the cheetah was flying past, the snail had no fear of not entering the ark. The snail knew Noah would wait for him. As you hear of what God has done for another, be certain of this—you are only one step away!

God Does New Things

What if you are believing God for something you have never heard done before? Who had a baby at ninety before Sarah? Who parted the Red Sea before Moses? Who made the sun stand still before Joshua? Yours can be the first. If science can come up with new discoveries or can have new inventions all the time or we ourselves seek to pioneer new things or become prodigies, cannot a big God who created *you* do something new? Think about it. Why do we limit Him so?

Remember, we have already examined this verse below in an earlier chapter. Why not meditate on it again? God loves to please His children. He wants to do something new in your life even now.

> *See, I am doing a new thing! Now it springs up; do you not perceive it? I am making a way in the desert and streams in the wasteland* (Isaiah 43:19).

Why would God want to do something new for you? Because you are unique. Even if you are a twin, there is no one like you or ever will be. God is certainly not about to run out of ideas!

Yes, testimonies are important. As has been said earlier, it was through the testimony of another brother in church who had survived a coma that Eze got to the final rung of his ladder. God bless the brother for sharing such a testimony!

How much has the Lord done for you to date? Telling our testimonies is one of the greatest witnesses of God today. We need to tell our communities, tell the nations how much the Lord has done for us. We need to amaze others with God's goodness. We have got to stir up the faith of the people, encourage them, and minister to them. We must preserve life as the salt of the earth (see Matt. 5:13). We must bring light to those dark areas.

And this we can do by our testimonies.

Closing Thoughts

Anything received miraculously by the Spirit of God must be kept by the Spirit. This is so important in keeping our healing. It is therefore important we go to God's Word to learn just how to do this, else we find ourselves in situations where we lose our healing and then doubt if God does truly perform miracles today. Yes, there are practical and natural things we must still do in order to aid the healing and recovery process. Some of these things include appropriate rest, but things of the Spirit must be dealt with as such.

Worth noting is that testimonies are the word of God. The Bible is full of testimonies, which we indeed call the Word. And what does the Word of God do? It transforms lives. The Word affects a person's spirit, soul, and body. The testimony you share, no matter how small, may be the thread that someone hangs onto for their life. Imagine if we never had testimonies of Hannah, Abraham, and Moses to name a few? Study Hebrews 11, which lists some of the most outstanding biblical testimonies. No, the devil will challenge your testimony, but you must stand. Oh yes, even if lying vanities of symptoms come back, keep sharing those testimonies. Those symptoms will eventually give. Outlast the devil through your testimonies. It is a sure and proven way of keeping your healing!

Summary

1. We overcome the devil when we share our testimonies.

2. We must share the full story and the full truth.

3. Ignore lying vanities and keep sharing your testimony. Eventually those lying vanities will permanently leave.

4. God can do something new for you even if He has never done it before. Ask God to give you a unique testimony.

Confession

I am not ashamed of what God has done in my life. Instead, I choose to bless others with the good news of God's miracles and power in my life. As I share my testimonies with others, they are strengthened. The devil is overcome in their lives as he is in mine. I give God the glory. In Jesus' name, amen.

Chapter Fourteen ————————————————————————————

EZE'S STORY

Recounting traumatic events is often not easy. However, the mindset one has certainly makes the difference. Getting the confidence of who I am in Christ means I can withstand the effects of any negative images. Jesus heals completely. And that includes numbing any emotional pain from negative memories. It includes healing the wounds without leaving the scars, which are painful reminders. God is neat!

Thank God, I also have the Counselor, the Holy Spirit, who has made it possible for me to pen my thoughts to you today without any feeling of remorse or sadness. Better than any counselor, the Holy Spirit is truly compassionate, caring, and deeply loving. Nothing separates us from the love of God (see Rom. 8:38-39). Like Paul, I am fully persuaded of His love. Even when it seemed dark and lonely, God was with me, loving and caressing me. Yes, He carried me.

My story started in February, 1992. Following the breakdown of a long-term relationship, a strong sense of loneliness had descended on me like a dark spirit. The loneliness, and also the move to the country of my birth (England) from the country where I was raised (Nigeria), translated into isolation.

It all started with a tetanus jab. A friend found me collapsed by my phone. Alerting my father by phone to Nigeria, we resolved that I would return to my parents and sort out my affairs in London later.

The friend took me to my bank to withdraw money for my flight and had to finish writing out my check after I had appended my signature. We went to a travel agent and booked a flight to Lagos for the following day. Not wanting to leave me on my own, I spent the night at his place and his brother took me to the airport the following morning. After he left, just as I was about to check in, I collapsed. The last thing I remember was hearing a woman screaming.

On gaining consciousness, I started hallucinating. I remember a series of policemen and later an ambulance as I was evacuated from the airport through the tarmac. I recall thinking while being taken into the ambulance that I was somehow still getting on the plane as other planes took off to the skies.

By this time, I had arrived at a destination and it dawned on me it was a hospital of sorts. An hour later, I was somehow feeling refreshed and started to tell the staff that I was meant to be traveling and requested that I be discharged so I could catch my flight. I seem to remember walking from one room to another in the hospital. I remember seeing blood on the floor in one room and a patient being held down by two people. I started getting worried. My thoughts were to leave, and I did in fact make an attempt to. I was instead prevented by several people who I later realized were porters. An injection was administered and I passed out into oblivion at this point.

I was eventually released into the care of my then pastor at the church I belonged to. My mother meanwhile flew into the UK within a week.

My story here is not meant to be a narrative, as the outline of my journey has already been told in the preceding chapters of this book. My journey to full health has, however, taught me to remain connected to the Source and to also understand that life is truly spiritual.

My journey led me to confess with my mouth that Jesus is Lord, believing in my heart that He was crucified for my sins and God raised Him from the dead (see Rom. 10:9). My journey led me to understand that God left the Holy Spirit on earth to continue His work through us believers. Thank God I found Jesus. Before this journey started, there was always a sense of suspended belief about the supernatural. But what would have been my story otherwise if I had never accepted Jesus as my Lord?

How did or how do I deal with the memories of the trauma of what I had been through, you may ask? Memories can hold you back in time if you let them. Paul said that he pressed forward toward the prize, forgetting all that is past. This means letting go of past failures and even successes and focusing on the purpose for our being. I knew I had a purpose. I had been an excellent student. Friends at school called me "Breeze" for the speed at which I grabbed information and retained it indefinitely. Even now, I still remember a great deal of things I learned in school.

But one cannot get emotional about the past or experiences. You see, emotions are tied to memories. To bring about the necessary change, I learned not to dwell on the past but to consistently and continually renew my mind through the Word of God and not allow unproductive thoughts.

Not accepting anything that the good Lord did not give me meant I developed a tenacity of mind and, very importantly, renewed my spirit. I never accepted the unspoken stigma of mental illness. Frankly, there was a sense of suspended disbelief as I carried on with life, always seeking for an end to medication.

But what about my self-image? Self-image affects self-esteem and relationships with others. My self-image was dented but never completely submerged by the journey. I had an optimism, a determination that kept me afloat. I remained barely buoyant in the hope that I would one day be my former self again.

To regain my self-image and my former popularity, I sought to remedy this by developing a social life outside work. I joined a social club and made new friends, hence helping with feelings of loneliness. I was given positions of responsibility in the club, and as people saw my capabilities I saw a flicker of hope. But the underlying issues had not been eliminated completely. If the root in a plant is not dug out and the branches are the only ones trimmed, the plant will keep growing. God is the only answer to uprooting evil roots!

Meeting my wife, Zoe, several years later was a turning point in my life. God brought her into my life at the right time. Of course, when a bachelor of many years like me eventually marries there are bound to be lots of changes. But in my case, these changes were important and life-changing ones.

My beautiful wife stood by me like spots on a leopard. She prayed me through. In fact, many nights she was up praying and studying the Word while I was long asleep. This beautiful woman cared for me with all her heart and soul. She showed me many things that had I had ceased seeing, issues that needed to be addressed but to which I was totally oblivious.

Honest feedback is essential for growth, and I finally got to get a constant dose of it with my wonderful wife. Trust is also essential. There is no human being I trust more than my wife, and this enabled me never to take any comments as a personal attack as I have always been trusting of her motives. I knew that she was helping me along this journey. I responded and in no time was seeing results. I learned to pray and study the Bible for one thing! My spiritual growth got a spurt—a good kicking. Zoe got me weaned off "Star Trek" and other television programs and instead got me watching Christian messages. She has been a rock who ensured that I consistently meditated on the Word of God, listened to messages regularly, and read Christian books. She did not buy clothes and shoes for herself, but rather bought Christian materials. We have so many books in our library and still counting! My life has become immersed in the Word, and my Christian walk is not a part of my life but *is* my life.

It is clear—if you are to win, you must be focused. You must invest your time wisely. There is no denying that the spiritual foundation is the only foundation that can give one the basis for a solid life. Thank God Zoe is a woman of God. Thank God that God had been preparing her over the years for the journey ahead. Thank God she answered the call to be my wife. A spirit-filled and spirit-controlled woman certainly makes a beautiful home!

Honesty with my wife was key to the way our relationship developed and the bond that held through the journey. My wife knew that if she asked me a question and insisted on an answer she would get the truth from me, and there are some things she knows it is not prudent to ask. She did not ask me what the diagnosis was and how many times I had been in the hospital, as it would affect her faith and color her perception of me. That is wisdom for someone growing their faith!

By the time my story ended, I had been on anti-psychotics for ten years and my body had grown very dependent on it. It would need a miracle to wean me off the drugs. Thank God I found Jesus and got that miracle. Through application of the Word and building my faith, I finally came off the medication and, most importantly, stayed off the medication. Even with the so-called stresses of life, I sailed through with no medication and no episodes.

So how did my story end?

I had weaned myself off the medication quite successfully for over a year. My work had requested a review by their own independent doctors who wrote to my personal doctor for my medical report. The report that came back highlighted that I was uncooperative in taking the daily pre-scribed drugs. They could see from the records I had not been in for a prescription in a while. Also, it was at this time that I found out that my medical report had that I was diagnosed with schizophrenia!

But all things work out for good to those who love God. Thank God I love God. Thank God His ways are not our ways. Thank God that through the Spirit we can unearth the ways of God. We can get this reve-lation knowledge of how God intends us to walk.

I submitted a request to my doctor's office, requesting to be re-viewed by a specialist in order to break this deadlock. I had not been assessed for a long time by now. That was how I ended up with the con-sultant psychiatrist who finally discharged me indefinitely. After two consultations with him of fact-finding, assessments, questions, and more questions, the consultant discharged me at the end of the second appointment, but not before also interviewing my wife, Zoe, too. Hearing the consultant concur that there was no evidence to support the previous diagnosis of schizophrenia was a defining moment for me. The consultant put the previous incidents down to internalizing stresses and recommended instead that I talk over stressful situations especially with my wife, who he agreed had played a large part toward reaching the end of this journey.

I could spend the rest of my life trying to work out if in fact a misdiag-nosis had ever been made all those years ago. Frankly, that is only one small part of this jigsaw puzzle. The fact is, whether or not it was so, God is still in the divine healing business. It means that no matter what the diagnosis is or how long you have been on a mountain, you can climb down and live a healthy, victorious life.

One thing I do know, however, is then when God does something, He does it to perfection and to completion. I am no longer labeled as schizo-phrenic. The final consultant who signed me off recorded instead that he would record the previous diagnosis as open. In other words, inconclusive.

My God meanwhile has a conclusion for this story. I am whole. I have a sound mind. What mystifies a doctor is of no effect to God who created me, the One who has even numbered the very hairs on my head. He knows me intimately. His Word penetrated parts medicine could not reach and broke the dependency of drugs in my body.

Only God could have done this. And now I have a beautiful story. Yes, I received a touch of that healing balm. I received a touch, and now I am whole.

Conclusion

God loves you. He has no favorites. What He did for Eze, He'll do for you. He is definitely no respecter of persons (see Acts 10:34).

Eze's and my faith in God's Word defied the odds. It defied the psychiatrists' reports. It defied the doctor's prognosis. On Eze's penultimate visit to the consultant psychiatrist who discharged him, the consultant actually asked Eze if he knew what schizophrenia was, as if to imply that the person who was seated opposite him, Eze, could not possibly have had such a disease. He even wrote to the psychiatrist who had first diagnosed Eze with this disease to ask for his reasons why such a diagnosis had ever been made.

But Jesus heals today. He certainly has not retired. And when Jesus does anything, it is with such perfection that it would cause men to marvel. God's healing will cause your doctor to go back to question whether a mistake was ever made in the first place.

Ours is not a testimony against the field of medicine. I mentioned at the beginning that we have a lot of respect for doctors. Luke, an apostle in the Bible, was a physician after all. Once again, this testimony is not advocating that you throw away your drugs. You have to reach that victory note in your spirit where your faith can allow yourself to take drastic measures. The demand of faith causes you to take a step of boldness. And when that faith is taken, faith will not let you down.

The woman with the issue of blood had faith that did not let her down, that did not cause her to be disappointed. Her faith had gone beyond human reasoning. What? Touching the hem of a garment to get healed? Where is the scientific evidence of this? Reasoning will nullify the power of God. But indeed that was what the woman with the issue of blood did. As she touched the garment of Jesus, there was a divine exchange. It was effective and immediate. This woman released her faith and in return was gloriously healed. Yes, she needed a physical point of contact in order to appropriate her healing, but it was her faith that made her whole.

What is your touch of faith today? The Word of God has the power to renew your mind and develop your faith. With the touch comes the corresponding healing power you desire. You see, anyone can have Eze's testimony too. I am not saying your healing from mental sickness may happen immediately or overnight, but it *will* happen if you keep flexing your faith muscles. That is not to say it cannot be instantaneous. Jesus healed the demon-possessed man at the Gerasenes immediately, didn't He? But don't feel condemned or guilty if you do not see an immediate change. Remember, ours is a story of little by little. Remember too that Eze suffered a few setbacks along the way. However, as you may recall, each setback was a springboard for his next level of healing.

Don't let spiritual pride stand in the way of receiving your healing. What is spiritual pride, you ask? Trusting that your faith is enough. Believing that you should be healed by the faith you have. Remember, there was still a key missing when Eze had his final attack. In order to stop the recurrent episodes, we needed to move up the next rung of the faith ladder.

Yes, Jesus said if we had faith as small as a mustard seed, we would be able to move mountains (see Matt. 17:20). But hear this—mountains come in different heights and altitudes. Not every mountain climber will attempt Everest. Likewise in our faith walk, in order to move certain mountains, we must grow our faith.

You see, there are times when God wants us to grow up. We must recognize those times. It is for our own good. In Hebrews 5:12, Paul was reprimanding the Christians for being slow in their growth. It is not good for us to remain as spiritual babes. Our president of our ministry says babes sin all the time. Grow up and know what is right. Remember the infirmed man who had been sick for thirty-eight years at the pool of Bethsaida (see John 5:5-8). Jesus warns him, "…you are well again. Stop sinning or something worse may happen to you" (John 5:14). Eze and I made ourselves relevant by being servants in the house of God. It is one way of growing up very quickly. We know how mature children can develop when we give them responsibilities, right? The same is true of spiritual matters too. Don't make yourself more susceptible to the enemy's attacks. Don't stay in ignorance and not know how to deal with him when he comes with his foolish nonsense! Get into the things of God instead.

Our road was not always smooth, as you know. If there are any set-backs of symptoms returning in your walk of faith, keep looking ahead. Don't get used to patterns of defeat. The devil, as stupid as he is, for example may say you cannot be healed. Don't believe the devil. He is after all the father of all lies (see John 8:44). Believe God instead. Remember the signpost of your destination is divine health. Don't camp anywhere else till you get there. Don't look at how far you have to go. Instead focus on how far you have come instead.

Finally, do not be bitter about your experiences, even during the period you suffered with mental illness. It does not matter how long it plagued your body. Let go of your past and share your testimony to help others. Move into the glorious future God has for you. As a child of God especially, you cannot lose. *All* things work together for good. Overcome the pain of your past and keep moving. Don't give up along the way. Don't consider the wasted years. Nothing is too late when it comes to God, though we must key in to get His perfect timing. He is neither a late God nor is He a sleeping God.

Certainly God has never lost a case. Yes, an eighteen-year journey finally came to an end. That means even the longest road has a turning.

We hope that this book has ministered to you. We certainly hope that this book has shown you that with God all things are possible. Keep your faith in God and stick with the Word.

And you will be sure to come back with a testimony. God bless you.

Salvation Prayer

If you have not received Jesus Christ as Lord of your life and would like to become a Christian, it is simple. All you have to do is say this simple prayer:

Heavenly Father, Your Word in Romans 10:13 says that those who call on the Lord will be saved. Your Word also says in Romans 10:9 that if we believe with our hearts and confess with our mouths that God raised Jesus from the dead, then we will be saved. I believe and now confess with my whole heart that God raised Jesus from the dead. I welcome the Holy Spirit to come and take up abode in my heart. I am now a new creation in Christ. Old things are passed away and behold I have become new (2 Cor. 5:17). I belong to a new family now. Thank You Jesus for this new glorious life. Thank You that You are now my Lord. I love You Lord. In Jesus' name, amen.

If you have said this prayer, make sure you find a Bible-believing church where the uncompromising Word of God is preached. The Bible says we must fellowship with other believers, so make it part of your lifestyle. As you do, you will defy the odds in life and come back with a testimony.

I would love to hear from you and how this book has blessed or encouraged you. Send your comments and prayers to:

defyingtheodds@live.co.uk

THE CROOKED PATHS

You are so gentle
Yet ever so prompting
You carry me through
Always in that thread
Of the Crooked Paths
That now and then run through my life

When I do not know what to do
Your Word teaches me.
You always get me to do
The right things
Making me realize that Crooked Paths
Are not necessarily
The Worst in life

Your Word straightens things in my mind,
My will and my emotions
Purifies my thoughts
Lets me stand
In the Power of Your might
Making the Crooked Paths straight

You taught me
To frame my world by the
Confessions of my lips
You have mapped out for me
The way I should go
Making the Crooked Paths straight

You've set people in my way
To guide me on the way
Ensuring that all things work
Together for my good
Because I love You . . .

Thank You Holy Spirit.

By Eze Onah

APPENDIX A

Surrey and Borders Partnership
NHS Foundation Trust

Tandridge Primary Care Mental Health Team
Langley House
Church Lane
Oxted
Surrey
RH8 9LH

Tel: 01883 385481
Fax:01883 385588

SR/jes
22nd March 2010

Dr ▓▓▓▓
Caterham Valley Medical Practice
Eothen House
Eothen Close
Caterham CR3 6JU

Dear Dr ▓▓▓▓

Re:	Eze Chukwuka ONAH – dob 2 ▓▓ – NHS: ▓▓▓▓	
GP: Dr ▓▓▓▓, Caterham Valley Practice		
Diagnosis:	No Mental Illness	ICD.10 Code:
Lead Professional	Dr ▓▓▓▓	
CPA Level	Statement of Care	
Risk	Low	
Medication/Care Plan	None	
Date of next Appointment	Discharged 19th March 2010	

I saw Mr Onah in my Outpatient Clinic on the 19th March 2010. He was accompanied by his wife.

He feels quite well in himself and his mood has remained stable for several months now. He expressed no particular concerns.

According to his wife there has been a significant change in him since a change in his lifestyle, particularly in the last six to eight months. He has become more outgoing and relates much better with the rest of the family and colleagues at work. His managers at work are also pleased with his improved performance and overall progress.

Mr Onah takes interest in his local church activities. He also plays the guitar and enjoys walking. He helps in the house with the housework.

He shows no evidence of mental illness. Both he and his wife are pleased with his overall progress.

I have today discharged him from the clinic back to your care but will be happy to see him again when necessary.

Best wishes,

Yours sincerely

Dr ▓▓▓▓
MBBS FRCPsych DPM
Consultant Psychiatrist

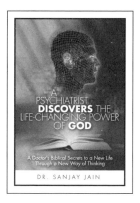

Additional copies of this book and other book titles from DESTINY IMAGE™ EUROPE are available at your local bookstore.

We are adding new titles every month!

To view our complete catalog online, visit us at:
www.eurodestinyimage.com

Send a request for a catalog to:

Via della Scafa, 29/14
65013 Città Sant'Angelo (Pe), ITALY
Tel. +39 085 4716623 • +39 085 8670146
info@eurodestinyimage.com

"Changing the world, one book at a time."

Are you an author?

Do you have a "today" God-given message?

CONTACT US

We will be happy to review your manuscript for the possibility of publication:

publisher@eurodestinyimage.com
http://www.eurodestinyimage.com/pages/AuthorsAppForm.htm